LITTLE FOREST FOLK

LITTLE FOREST FOLK

How to Raise Happy, Healthy Children who Love the Great Outdoors

LEANNA BARRETT

HarperCollins*Publishers*

HarperCollins*Publishers*
1 London Bridge Street
London SE1 9GF

www.harpercollins.co.uk

HarperCollins*Publishers*
Macken House, 39/40 Mayor Street Upper
Dublin 1, D01 C9W8, Ireland

First published by HarperCollins*Publishers* 2023

13 5 7 9 10 8 6 4 2

© Leanna Barrett 2023
Illustrations © Ollie Mann

Leanna Barrett asserts the moral right to
be identified as the author of this work

A catalogue record of this book
is available from the British Library

ISBN 978-0-00-858647-8

Printed and bound in the UK using 100%
renewable electricity at CPI Group (UK) Ltd

This book is produced from independently certified FSC™ paper
to ensure responsible forest management.

For more information visit: www.harpercollins.co.uk/green

To my husband and children

Contents

Introduction   1

Chapter 1   The Theory: Why is Nature so Important
for Our Children   11

Chapter 2   The Practicalities: Feel Empowered to
Get Outdoors, Whatever the Weather   27

The Activities:

Chapter 3   Activities for Spring   37

Chapter 4   Activities for Summer   75

Chapter 5   Activities for Autumn   115

Chapter 6   Activities for Winter   155

Epilogue   191

Appendix   193

Acknowledgements   195

About the Author   197

Introduction

I grew up in south Wales, enjoying a life very different from the experience of childhood that today's children are living through. My childhood was typical of the 1980s. We would regularly head out to play in the local fields, ponds and other natural areas, going out for an adventure without our parents and returning when it was time for tea. Children don't have that essential freedom to roam and play unsupervised today that we were fortunate enough to enjoy. Research by Mayer Hillman at the Policy Studies Institute suggests that in a single generation, from 1971 to 1990, the 'home habitat' of a typical eight-year-old – the area in which children are able to travel on their own – had shrunk to one ninth of its former size. Imagine the results if this study was conducted again today. I took the freedom I had for granted and, as an adult, didn't ever consider how much the world might have changed from my own childhood.

My eyes were first opened to how different things are for today's children when I had my first child. My daughter changed my world, as all children do. Seeing the world through her eyes, watching her grow was such a special experience. It changed who I am and my priorities in life.

Suddenly, all I wanted for this special little girl was for her to grow up connected to the natural world, in a way that was effortless when we were growing up in the seventies and eighties but which in 2011 seemed more difficult to achieve. I wanted her to know herself, to have time to explore, to investigate, and to learn all about the wonderful world we inhabit. I had to be realistic about the world we live in now and make this happen for her in a way that suited the times we are living in.

In 2012 I returned to work following my maternity leave and couldn't find an early years' education experience that delivered what I wanted for my child, one that mirrored the holistic and natural upbringing she was experiencing at home. My husband James and I lived in a small terraced house in London but were lucky enough to have a garden. As soon as my daughter could crawl, she would almost constantly move to the kitchen door and bang on it to communicate that she wanted to go into the garden. We went for long walks, visited parks and local woodland, spending most of our days outdoors. Those early days with your first baby can be exhausting and busy. For me, getting outdoors with my girl always made every day better.

My daughter loved the sensory aspect of being outdoors; she greatly enjoyed playing with soil and plants before developing an absolute fascination with insects and other small creatures. She noticed all of the small changes in the world that passed me by as a busy adult – the changing colours of the leaves, a weed or a flower popping up on the street, a snail on the pavement – and would crouch for hours to observe and play with the natural world.

James and I explored the option of moving to Scandinavia, where life seemed to more closely follow my principles. However, with our second baby on the way we decided to bite the bullet and stay put, to build our dream childhood for our children, by creating an early years' educational experience grounded in awe, wonder and inspiration, one with a direct and regular connection to the natural world. And so, Little Forest Folk was born.

In January 2015, we launched a full-time outdoor forest nursery for two- to five-year-olds in Wimbledon. We made the decision to launch Little Forest Folk in winter to show how, even in the depths of January, children dressed well and appropriately would thrive spending their days outdoors under the careful and skilful supervision of our early years' educators. Little Forest Folk was a unique concept where children could be dropped off at an indoor building (a scout hall) between 8 a.m. and 9 a.m., then be transported across to a local woodland where we would spend most of the day, Monday to Friday, 9.30 a.m. to 3.30 p.m., all year round, interacting with nature and playing outdoors. We had tents available for nap times, and portable toilets and nappy changing tents as our facilities.

The natural environment was our classroom, full of magic, inspiration, awe and wonder.

The children adored outdoor learning, developed astonishingly well, and consequently the awards and plaudits flooded in. Parents visiting our nursery found it a really emotive setting, which often made them wistful for their own childhood. Watching two-year-olds using tools and three-year-olds busily roasting marshmallows around the campfire, it seemed that this sense of calm and connectivity was the lifestyle they wanted for their entire family. We had lots of requests from parents and carers who wanted to stay on, to be a part of the experience, reliving their own childhood by playing in a forest, reconnecting with nature. We received a letter from Sir David Attenborough saying how children would look back in later years and realise how important their time with us was.

We were busy but thrilled at how magical an experience we were providing for children. By now with our third child, demand was rapidly surpassing what we could provide with one nursery. With the support of the Big Venture Challenge, who supported us as social entrepreneurs, we rapidly scaled up and by 2021 had seven nurseries in southwest London in order to reach even more families.

As I blinked, my children grew and were suddenly in their primary years. I wanted them to continue to enjoy an education that kept them connected to the natural world, which developed their passion and enthusiasm for environmentalism, which nurtured their emotional intelligence. I dedicated time to supporting their positive mental health and personal, social and emotional development, alongside empowering them to make good decisions and develop their self-regulation skills. I knew this didn't need to come at the cost of an academically rigorous and challenging curriculum. Children love to be challenged, if the challenge is authentic and real to them. If learning feels relevant and purposeful to a child then they have the self-motivation to persevere in overcoming academic challenges and to be resilient. Happy, secure children with a strong sense of well-being strive to learn deeply and meaningfully in all areas of the curriculum, not only building on their knowledge and skills but building self-esteem at the same time.

Little Forest Folk was the start of an incredible educational experience for my children and the others that attended, one during which they became independent and confident lifelong learners. They were creative, curious, empathetic and generally incredible little people. Their strong character and life skills developed through their freedom of time and space as they immersed themselves in the natural world. They were children who could make good decisions and choices in life through having had the freedom to make choices and decisions at nursery. They were children who were able to manage their own risk, through having learned to risk assess and work out their personal limits as they engaged in risky play, in a safe and secure environment.

I wanted my children to develop personally, but also to be academically challenged, through learning experiences that felt meaningful, purposeful and relevant to their lives. I didn't want their learning to be something that didn't feel deeply and richly connected to their lives. I wanted them to continue to feel a connection to the natural world and through this gain an understanding of their place in the world. I wanted them to feel socially responsible and have an awareness of their impact on the world and how it can be an extremely positive one; to be equipped not only with knowledge, but with the skills, attributes and lifelong character traits that would open every door their hearts desired and set them up to thrive and be successful in the twenty-first century.

As with my search for an early years' educational experience that met my high expectations, when the time came I couldn't find anything that matched my vision for primary age schooling for my children. My eldest daughter had gone off to school and I could sense her changing. I could see her creativity becoming more subdued, her questioning reduced as she began adapting to her school environment by becoming a girl who answered questions instead of asking them. I could see all of those life skills she had developed through her time in Little Forest Folk nursery being eroded. This was a local school, so the sense of community with other parents was lovely. It was an easy option for me to walk her 200 metres up the road to drop her off, socially it was a lovely school, and yet ...

Through my work at Little Forest Folk, I frequently attended education conferences where experts from around the world shared research and evidence into what children truly need from their education to set them up to thrive in life. I wanted to continue the journey the children had been on in my nurseries thus far and to strengthen their emotional well-being, their character and life skills, their love of learning, their connection to the natural world and their freedom to play. I used to cry at least once in every conference as time and time again speakers discussed a beautiful pedagogy that was absolutely present in my nurseries and in schools across the world, but which I knew my own daughter was not experiencing.

The thought of opening a school was overwhelmingly daunting. I spent at least a year wishing the school of my dreams would be created by someone else. I hoped and I waited, until the weight of feeling constantly that my daughter (and my rapidly growing son and second daughter) deserved more outweighed my apprehension about starting a school. So, I dug deep and once again created something that didn't exist. I am now the proud head of Liberty Woodland School in Morden, southwest London; a school which is developing my own and other children to be the best version of themselves. Children at my school learn predominantly outdoors, with cosy sheltered dens, an art studio and other sheltered spaces available for use when required. We have a 3-acre glorious site where our children are free to 'be' in the natural world. On a recent autumn day, I asked a range of children (from the four-year-olds right up to 12-year-olds) what made Liberty Woodland School special. They all answered along the same theme: being in nature, hearing the birds sing, being able to be around trees. When I followed up their answers by asking them how being in nature all day made them feel, without any discussion between them and without hesitation they almost all answered 'calm and happy'. If we don't start from this basis, if we don't ensure children are calm, happy and feeling safe, learning doesn't work, connections don't happen, well-being and mental health are affected. I know that to set children up for success in life, personal, social and emotional development must be an absolute priority. Our school children spend dedicated time every day working on these skills, which means they are developing emotional intelligence that will last them a lifetime.

At Liberty Woodland School we work actively to develop the life skills that children need to thrive in the twenty-first century. We are a re-imagining of school. Our academically rigorous work is meaningful, relevant and purposeful to the children through our project-based learning. As I've said, children can, and will, strongly pursue their own learning when it means something to them. Our passionate and hard-working children have an ethic of excellence in their work and achieve great things. By keeping well-being at the heart of everything we do, we have pupils who feel so secure, safe, grounded and happy that they can be really challenged academically, and find this rigorous challenge fun rather than daunting. I can't wait to see the impact of Liberty Woodland School on these children as they develop into young adults.

In 2022, my eldest daughter turned 11 years old and Liberty Woodland School extended to provide secondary school education. We chose to use the academically rigorous International Baccalaureate curriculum as the foundation of our learning as we feel it is far more appropriate for the modern world. Through the IB we are able to develop young people to achieve great success academically in order for them to pursue the next phase of their lives, while also ensuring we don't let go of our strong focus on mental health, social skills, emotional well-being, entrepreneurship and communication. As part of the move to launch Liberty Woodland School Secondary, it was time for James and I to sell Little Forest Folk so that my focus could be solely on developing Liberty Woodland School. I'm happy to say that Little Forest Folk is still going, under new ownership and with my core staffing teams still intact.

Parents joke that my next step will be to open Liberty Woodland University when my children reach the age of 18. However, they are on their own from then on – I know they will be prepared for anything and everything that comes their way in life.

My mission now, alongside my running of Liberty Woodland School Primary and Secondary, is to reach more children than ever before, to share the fascinating research and journey we have been on over the past eight years and to inspire more parents to take their children back outdoors. I know how challenging time and logistics can be when you are a parent or carer, so I want to try and make life as simple for you as possible by sharing some of my learning from the past eight years and to provide some shortcuts to help you create a positive childhood for your family in the great outdoors. I know that not everyone can attend or would want to attend an outdoor school, so I hope to provide ways to make this style of learning and living accessible to all families, whether it be on weekends, after school or even offering you a different way of viewing the world as you walk to school.

1.

The Theory
Why is Nature so Important for Our Children

The benefits of a deep and regular connection to the natural world cannot be overstated. There has never been a research project conducted that doesn't evidence how powerful time in nature can be. There are direct correlations between the amount of time spent in nature and strong mental health, overall well-being and physical development. In this chapter, I would like to expand on the many benefits children will reap from increased time spent playing in and exploring natural environments.

Happiness

Unleashing the instinct to play will make our children happier, more self-reliant, and better students for life.

PETER GRAY, FREE TO LEARN

Parenting is exhausting. There are now so many choices and opinions on childhood and how it should be spent, and I'm aware I am offering just another opinion. There are so many activities available for children to enjoy. Parenting has become almost competitive, not necessarily from a desire to win but from a desire to not miss out and not deny your child opportunities in life. But if we break down a parent's core dream for their child, isn't it for them to be happy, to show interest in the world around them and be motivated to learn?

In the mental health pandemic we are living through in the UK, it has become undeniable that without positive mental and emotional well-being, without personal fulfilment and feeling a connection to the world, without happiness, achieving all the success in the world doesn't matter.

If I think about any time in my life, from those exhausting early baby days to busier older children, one thing that was guaranteed to make any day better was stepping outside. Stepping outside doesn't have to mean you need a forest in your back garden, or a nature reserve at the end of your street. Often just stepping outside your front door can bring that instant feeling of relief from tension. Being outdoors and taking a deep breath of fresh air is one of the fastest ways to improve health and happiness. Simply being outside, ideally in nature, has been shown to lower stress levels, blood pressure and your heart rate, while encouraging physical activity and buoying mood and mental health. Another bonus point for stepping outside, of course, is that it's free!

In addition to lowering your cortisol levels – our body's main stress hormone, too much cortisol challenges your ability to maintain positive physical and mental health – and generating feelings of calm, spending time outdoors in nature makes you feel grounded. There has been enough research now that health professionals have begun to prescribe time outdoors to improve well-being. Even 10 minutes in nature has been found to make you feel happier and lessen mental stress. Being outdoors in nature makes us feel more connected to ourselves, and more connected to the natural world, which helps us to feel secure in knowing our place in the world.

Don't feel like you have to dramatically change your life, you can start small. Begin by going outdoors every day and not rushing to school/the shops/wherever you usually race to. Leave early to allow for time to wonder and be curious along your way. Head outdoors and follow your child's lead, and your child's pace. The years with our children fly by in a flash; if we slow down our lives to follow our child's pace, we may be able to see the world through their astonished eyes. Take the time to observe how even small changes such as a flower budding make you feel and to support your child in doing the same. Observe changes in your child's behaviour as they become more grounded, more observant, live more in the moment and are more connected with the world. I know as a working mum myself that for many of you time will be your most precious commodity, so it's difficult to do this. If time is indeed so valuable, shouldn't it be the thing we prioritise giving to our children above all else? I often have to remind myself to just ... slow ... down.

In an increasingly busy world, where life is interconnected, fast and constantly changing, time spent in nature can be a constant throughout childhood. A familiar experience, and one which through connection to the immediate natural environment can provide children with a sense of stability and an awareness of their place in the world. These will be the memories that last. These will be the memories of their best days.

Creativity

Creativity is seeing what others see and thinking what no one else has ever thought.

ALBERT EINSTEIN

In 1992 NASA asked Dr George Land and Beth Jarman to develop a highly specialised test that would allow them to effectively measure the creative potential of NASA's rocket scientists and engineers. The test was designed to identify employee's capacity for divergent thinking and creativity to allow NASA to hire the best of the best. It was a very effective test for NASA's purposes, but things got really interesting when scientists considered the theory of nature vs nurture. Are certain people born with a strong sense of creativity, or can creativity be learned from life experiences or be taught? The results from the NASA study were that 98 per cent of four- to five-year-olds were considered creative geniuses. In the same group of children, by age six 30 per cent were considered creative geniuses. By age 12 the number had dropped to 12 per cent whereas by adulthood less than 2 per cent of these creative geniuses still tested as creative geniuses. This study seems to confirm the theory of Sir Ken Robinson – one of the world's most famous educationalists who has written numerous books and presented inspiring talks on this subject – that schools kill creativity. Creativity is one of the most in-demand skills of the twenty-first century. We must not allow education to kill it.

We want children to develop, rather than lose, the amazing capacity for creativity they were born with. We want children to see questions, rather than learning to recite answers. We want children upon being asked a question to maintain the ability to see a multitude of possible answers. If they can't see a multitude of answers, then we want them to possess the ability to think creatively and independently about where they might be able to seek them. We want children to think outside of the box. This is how the best and most creative solutions can be found to the most challenging problems in society.

Spending time in nature has a magical ability to switch on our creativity; it makes us more curious, makes us question, makes us notice and encourages us to explore. New ideas are sparked and through the unpredictability of nature our imaginations are ignited as we begin to explore new possibilities.

One of the things that blew visitors' minds when they came along to visit the Little Forest Folk nurseries is how little in terms of resources children need to be happy. Indeed how much happier children can be with less. The old adage of children often preferring the cardboard box the toy came in to the actual toy is proven accurate time and time again when children find sticks, mud, trees and the natural environment an inspiration for hours of creative play. Less is often more. A toy with fancy light-up buttons and sounds only plays one way and can get boring quickly. A cardboard box, a stick, some mud, a piece of fabric, sand, stones, water, a pile of conkers ... these open-ended resources can be anything and everything. Open-ended resources can fluctuate and adapt according to the ebb and flow of play. Open-ended play provides endless opportunities for creativity and critical thinking skills, often along with being social and rich with communication.

Children don't need more possessions. The advertising world is constantly bombarding both children and adults with the message that we need more stuff. Spending money on new toys is not the answer. Use fewer things and use those you have in a better way. Use nature. When you do shop, use charity shops and eBay. It's about experiences, not possessions. Really think about whether or not you need to buy that toy for your child, particularly toys that offer only one way of playing. If a toy tells a child how to play, if an activity tells a child what or how to create, we are teaching them that they don't need to think for themselves. You can create an alternate world where natural open-ended resources, or even open-ended toys, allow children to see the amazing power of their minds through exploring their own imaginations and creativity. Boxes of fabric, loose parts and cardboard boxes can provoke hours of rich and imaginative play.

The play will change over time as your children grow. My children, now aged seven, nine and 11, still enjoy playing with cardboard-box creations, but in a very different way from when they were two years old. If your child struggles initially to play with open-ended resources, take them outdoors and teach them to patiently observe the world around them; begin with nature or use the hook of their favourite book or activity to ease them into open-ended play.

Let children wander aimlessly, let them wonder, leave them to their imaginations, their relationships and the natural world and watch to see the explosion of magical creative inspiration that will follow. There is little more fascinating than the ever-changing natural world. Slow down as you walk; even on the streets children will notice the changes in their environment as the seasons change and time passes. Celebrate these discoveries and observations with them. Share the wonder of their observations and enjoy how attuned they are to the world around them. Adults can learn so much from children.

Independence, confidence and resilience

The greatest gifts you can give your children are the roots of responsibility and the wings of independence.

DENIS WAITLEY

The greatest gift you can give your child, alongside time with a loving parent or carer, is the freedom of their own time and space. It's difficult to resist the urge to fill your child's schedule with all that is on offer, but factoring time to just relax and be is critically important too.

In our fast-paced world, it's more important than ever to ensure your child has time to sit, to ponder, to relax, to ground themselves in the world – and even time to be bored. If children move from being directed by adults at school all day to being directed by adults at after-school clubs and activities on evenings and weekends, they will never have

time to foster independence, to
feel genuine agency over their
own happiness and well-being as
they learn to manage boredom
and develop their creativity
through doing so.

   Children need as much time
as possible to be self-directed,
not adult led. Rather than
trying to mould children into
the kind of adults we believe will be successful, by creating a
desirable mix of skills and characteristics, we should focus on
creating nurturing environments. To provide the conditions
for children to flourish and grow into their own independent
individuals. Children are astonishingly capable and wonderful
people. We need to let them, and trust them, to self-direct.

   Autonomy, not dependence. We have progressed to a
society where 18-year-olds struggle to make decisions, yet is
this any wonder when childhood and young adulthood is now
so adult-directed that it's possible these 18-year-olds have
never had the opportunity to develop these independent skills.

   Children can sense authenticity a mile off. For them to feel
empowered and learn to make decisions for themselves, we
have to offer them genuine trust and faith in their abilities
to manage themselves. Then, if you're anything like me, step
back and cross your fingers! In our experiences at Liberty
Woodland School, having high expectations of children
consistently develops children who rise and often surpass
your expectations of them.

Try not to be persuaded through competitive parenting to overschedule children, and through this spend money you don't need to spend, if it's not what is best for your family. What your child needs, what your child wants, is time with you, experiences with you. Think back to your own childhood – are your most vivid memories of attending chess clubs, or tennis clubs? Or are they of kneeling next to ponds, fishing tadpoles with siblings or parents, or playing in the streets with your friends?

The trips to theme parks and expensive days out bring their own stresses and the expectation that as something has cost a lot of money, everyone should really enjoy it. A walk in the park with some inspiring props to spark off play can be so much more relaxing, more engaging for children and more enjoyable for the whole family. And free!

Let's give young children the childhood they deserve. Provide them with opportunities to play outdoors, in natural environments, with the gifts of freedom of time and space. The numerous research studies conducted on this prove unequivocally that free play in nature fosters self-confidence, builds resilience, develops independence, encourages 'safe' risk-taking alongside developing the ability to risk assess, and strongly develops problem-solving skills.

In order to foster children who will thrive in today's constantly changing world, we must give them freedom to play, ideally in nature. Children, and indeed even young animals, have a biological need to play. Play is the child's way of working to develop into an effective adult and is the primary means of practising the intellectual skills that will be needed in later life. Play, genuine play, not a game directed by adults, or an activity designed by an adult to achieve a specific outcome, is the foundation of social and emotional development. Where possible, provide children with friends/ siblings to play with, provide safe supervision, but then step back and allow them to explore the wonderful world we live in and begin their rehearsals for life.

Wonder lives in every child. Every child has the capability of being extraordinary. Wisdom begins in wonder. The wonders of nature are endless. Provide children with the gift of knowing their place in the universe and with feeling secure with their connection to the natural world.

The weather

Something we can't not discuss in a book about embracing the natural world, is the weather! There's a famous adage that says 'There's no such thing as bad weather, only bad clothing.' Please don't restrict yourself to outings only on sunny, warm days. If you do, you are missing out on a myriad of opportunities.

We are so fortunate in the UK to not really have extreme weather conditions, or not yet anyway. Take advantage of the fact that it is rarely too hot or too cold to go outside and head out no matter the weather. How great a way is it to build your child's resilience, not through adverse experiences but by simply being outdoors when it's a bit wet, or cold, or snowy? How amazing to develop your child into someone who doesn't spend their life waiting for sunny days, but embraces each and every day as an opportunity to experience wonder and find joy. Often on those cold or wet days, it's getting outside that's the challenge. If you can find the energy to get you and your family out of the front door, properly dressed, then even the shorter days of winter sunshine still have enough daylight to raise your vitamin D levels, boost your immune system and reduce your cortisol levels.

It's hard to create new habits and new ways of life, so start small. Don't feel that to be a truly outdoors family you need to rug up for full-day expeditions every time you head out. Being outdoors with your child shouldn't be an endurance test. Keep every experience a positive experience by planning for what is realistic and achievable for your family. Some soggy days in winter we just head out for a one-hour walk, going to a new destination to make the walk more attractive and enticing. Be kind to yourself and keep it simple, short and successful. You can build up everyone's tolerance for being outdoors in more adverse weather.

Environmentalism and social responsibility

No one will protect what they don't care about; and no one will care about what they have never experienced.

SIR DAVID ATTENBOROUGH

A deep and regular connection develops children into the future custodians of the planet. We have in our children the generation who are going to change the world. They are the generation who *have* to change the world. The situation we are handing down is terrifying. While us parents are still coming to grips with the severity of the climate disaster looming ahead of us and already present for large swathes of the world, while we are trying to fully accept the reality of the future and begin work on changing our behaviours to give our children a fighting chance of a stable future, they seem to intuitively understand the challenges we are facing.

Children who feel a deep connection to the natural world instinctively and naturally want to protect it. From their early days of carefully relocating a snail from the pavement to the safety of the bushes along the side of the road, children's natural drive to protect their world progresses from care of minibeasts and flowers to picking up litter, to working on increasing biodiversity, through to advocating for renewable energy. This generation possesses such a drive to save the world that if we arm them with the skills and knowledge they need, they can turn this drive into a force for change.

Teaching children about environmentalism and sustainability from a young age ensures that their attachment to the natural environment becomes embedded as a force for change through their behaviour. There are great books on the subject out there if you want to read to your child from a young age, such as *Climate Action* by Georgina Stevens and *The Great Big Green Book* illustrated by Ros Asquith. These books will allow children to begin to understand the power they have to change the world for the better. I will be recommending other inspirational reads throughout.

Many of the activities I recommend can start to foster this real sense of social responsibility and allow children to feel empowered to create positive change. Parents and carers should provide children with concrete ways they can contribute to society positively. Narrate their actions to them when they seize opportunities to make a difference. Support them in their drive to make the world a better place.

Many parents are concerned about children experiencing eco-anxiety as they themselves are feeling the pressure of the climate crisis. At Liberty Woodland School, environmentalism is one of the core skills we teach as we believe it is crucial to equip these passionate young people with the skills and knowledge they need to have a positive impact on the climate crisis. From

our environmentalism teacher, I recently learned about the work of child psychologist Caroline Hickman who believes we should re-frame 'eco-anxiety' as 'eco-empathy or eco-compassion' as this is a 'healthy response to the situation we are facing', because it shows awareness of the problem and a willingness to face the challenge of solving it.

I am also inspired by Kate Marvel, NASA climate scientist, who said: 'As a climate scientist, I'd like you to know: I don't have hope. I have something better: certainty. We know exactly what's causing climate change.
We can absolutely 1) avoid the worst and 2) build a better world in the process.'

I believe we can inspire and develop our young people to be the future custodians of the planet and be the generation who solves the problem of the climate crisis.

2.

The Practicalities
Feel Empowered to Get Outdoors, Whatever the Weather

Some of you will live in the countryside, with nature surrounding you. Others, like me, live in a city. Some will have gardens, or an easy connection to a little bit of green space; others won't. Wherever you live, you can adapt your lifestyle to feel more connected to the natural world, and to share a deep and regular connection to nature with your child. In this chapter, I want to show you how easy it can be to bring nature into your family life, whether you have acres of woodland at the back of your garden or you live in a block of flats without any outdoor space.

Dress for success

The most important contributor to a successful outing into nature with your child is preparation. Check the weather forecast and dress accordingly. It's worth investing in good-quality clothing as being warm is so important. A warm and dry child is a happy child, one who will be happy to explore the great outdoors for hours.

Different seasons require different clothing, but successful outdoor dressing is all about the layers. Always try to choose fabrics and sizes that allow for air to move between the layers as it's the trapped air that keeps you warm. It also allows you to peel off or add a layer as required. At all times of year, I would recommend carrying spare clothes. Always throw an extra jumper, hat, socks and gloves into a bag as once your extremities get cold or wet, it's hard to warm up. If you're planning a puddle-jumping expedition, pop some spare trousers in too. And on cold days, don't forget to tuck your thermal tops into your thermal trousers for extra warmth!

You'll find a list of recommended and trusted clothing brands I recommend at the back of the book. Good-quality outdoor clothing will outlast how quickly a child grows. Don't forget to try charity shops and online marketplaces too. Buying second-hand clothing is not only better for your budget but also for the environment. And do pass things on – outdoor clothing, boots and bag hand-me-downs pass around my friends and family constantly.

Here is a list, more or less by season, of the basics I'd recommend. These are designed around a British climate, so adapt if you are in a warmer or colder climate.

EARLY-MID SPRING

- Fitted thermal long-sleeve top
- Thermal trousers
- T-shirt
- Leggings/trousers
- Thick jumper
- Wellies or snow boots/hiking boots
- Thin socks
- Thick socks
- Waterproof trousers/dungarees
- Waterproof jacket

MID-SPRING TO EARLY SUMMER

- Short-sleeve T-shirt
- Leggings/trousers
- Warm jumper
- Wellies
- Thin socks
- Waterproof trousers/dungarees
- Waterproof jacket

SUMMER TO EARLY AUTUMN

- Short-sleeve T-shirt
- Shorts/trousers/leggings
- Thin socks
- Closed-toe shoes
- Waterproof trousers/dungarees
- Waterproof jacket
- Sun hat

AUTUMN

- Short- or long-sleeve T-shirt
- Leggings/trousers
- Warm jumper
- Wellies or snow boots/hiking boots
- Thin socks
- Waterproof trousers/dungarees
- Waterproof jacket

WINTER

- Fitted thermal long-sleeve top
- Looser thermal long-sleeve top

- Thin jumper
- Thick jumper
- Long-sleeve T-shirt
- Fleece-lined leggings/trousers
- Thermal trousers
- Hiking boots or snow boots (wellies do not keep little toes warm in winter)
- Thin socks
- Thick socks
- Waterproof trousers/dungarees
- Warm ski-style jacket or warm jacket with a thin waterproof jacket on top
- Woollen beanie hat
- Scarf or snood
- Gloves

Snacks and refreshments

Essential to the success of a day in the great outdoors is to ensure you have plenty of snacks and drinks with you. Nothing can derail a fun family outing more than hungry tummies and the incessant demanding of snacks. I like to take snacks that are portable yet filling, using pulses, oats, seeds, nuts etc. to ensure maximum tummy-filling impact from each.

A quality, insulated water bottle (it's worth investing in one that doesn't leak), a thermos flask and bamboo cups (portable and lightweight but avoiding the use of plastic) will set you up nicely for outdoor adventures. I also recommend getting something like a Yumbox, if it's an option for you.

These are expensive and feel extravagant, but are a really great way to carry a variety of foods and snacks with minimal packaging and weight. Mine are some of my most used picnic items. You can often pick up second-hand lunch boxes like these on eBay as they last for ever.

Appropriate drinks can help to elevate the adventure – from hot chocolate in winter to warm and refuel your little companions, to a refreshing homemade lemonade or fruit slushie on a hot day. Something that feels decadent and special as a reward will certainly help add an incentive for tired legs to keep walking for a little longer.

Remember, a warm, dry child with a full tummy is always going to enjoy an adventure outdoors so much more and so it's worth the prep of dressing well and packing snacks. And a happy child almost always makes for a more enjoyable outing for everyone!

How to plan an adventure walk

All year round, one of my favourite things to do with young ones is to go on an adventure walk. We started to use this phrase in our nurseries when children wanted to explore a wider area of the natural environment than the section of woodland in which their nursery was located. It soon became one of their favourite parts of the day. An adventure walk is a walk, steered by children, that doesn't necessarily have a destination in mind. It is a walk that can be taken at any pace, with plenty of time to stop and explore, play or investigate along the way.

Where are your nearest parks? Scout around, open a map of your local area and just look for patches of green near your home. Then go and explore. This will not only be a fun adventure-walk activity but will also help you to find magical hidden spots of nature for further adventures.

Preparation for adventure walks follow the same principles as always, of dressing for success and carrying snacks and drinks, but for adventure walks I always take along a few resources which could extend the experience. Your best resources to play with and explore can be found in the natural world around you. Picking up a stick along the way can provide hours of fun. I like to take some additional resources on longer walks or days when I'm tired and feel I need something extra tucked away as a provocation; simply adding some of these resources can extend play enormously.

Optional adventure walk resources (as recommended by my children):

- Binoculars
- Magnifying glass
- Bug jar
- Double-sided sticky tape
- Chalk
- Clipboard and paper and pens
- Twine and/or a rope
- Scissors
- Pond-dipping net is also a must-take

Optional inspirational read:

- *Tiny, Perfect Things* by M. H. Clark

The Activities

Process not Product

I have offered suggestions for activities to get you started on your journey to being an outdoors family, but please see these as suggestions and ideas rather than a list of must-follow instructions. So often children will have far better ideas than me of crafts you can make or adventures you can enjoy with a small bundle of resources. The most beautiful outdoor learning is all about the process, not the product.

Don't worry too much if your child's raft turns into an aeroplane, or if your clay hedgehog develops into a clay worm. Your end products may not be perfect, and they may not be what you started out planning to create. This doesn't matter. Just enjoy the creative journey and the shared nature-play experience with your child. A wonky product at the end of an activity is all part of the fun!

Key to Icons

My recommended activities can take place anytime and anywhere, but as a guide I've included some icons to explain where they might be best suited to.

 Your home or a balcony (although you may need to access an outside space to collect materials)

 A garden

 The park

 A forest or woodland

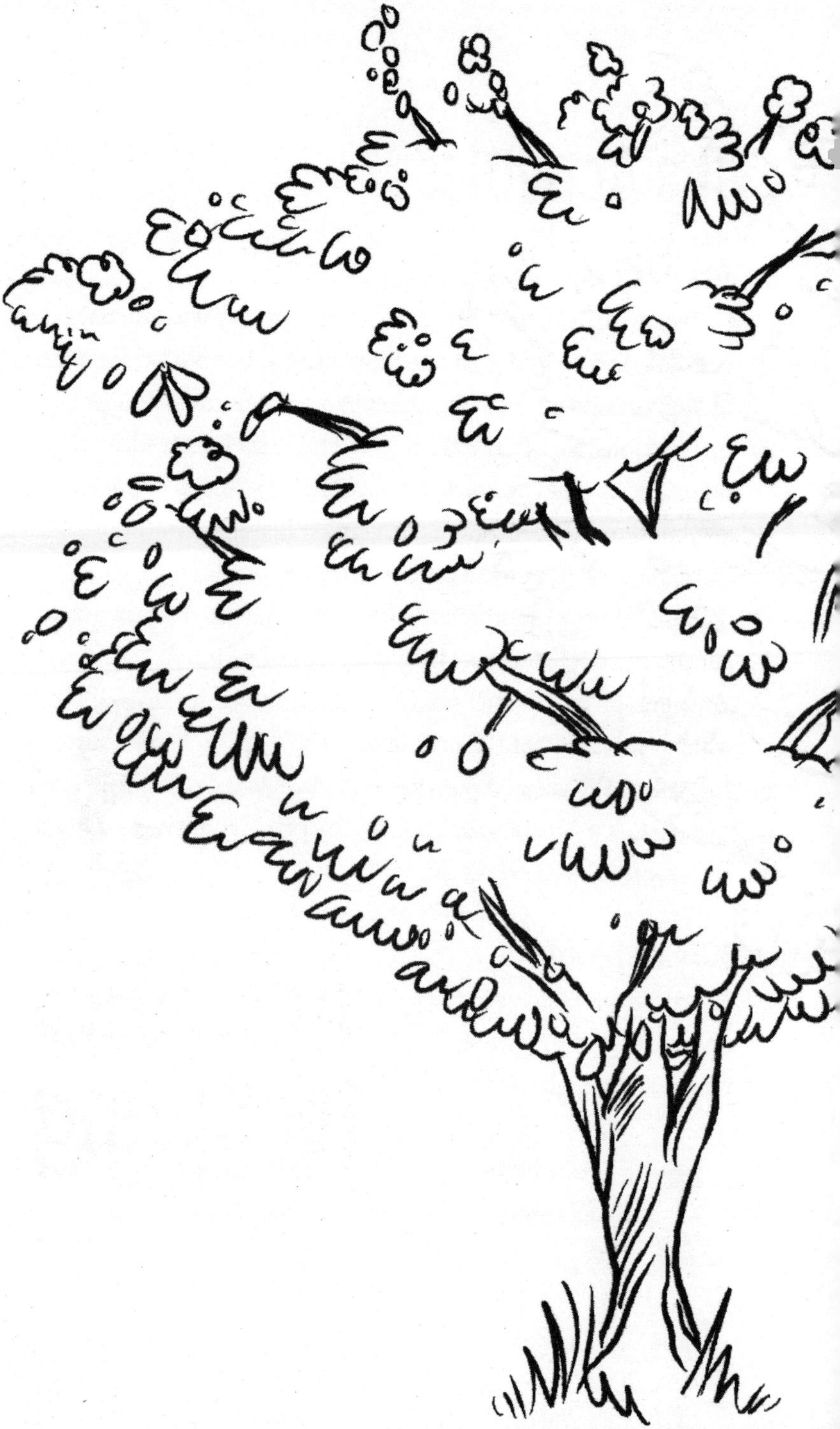

3.
Activities
for Spring

Build a mini bug hotel

My daughter simply loves insects. From a very young age she would regularly explore the garden, the forest or even the pavement, and forage under logs, bricks and sticks looking for woodlice, slugs, snails and worms. She would name them and do her best to make sure they were happy and comfortable.

An extension of this exploration is creating a mini bug hotel. This activity provides an opportunity to learn more about little creatures, to counteract the loss of natural habitat in our world, and help the natural environment by creating a safe space for insects to shelter, lay their eggs and raise their young. It develops empathy and compassion in your child

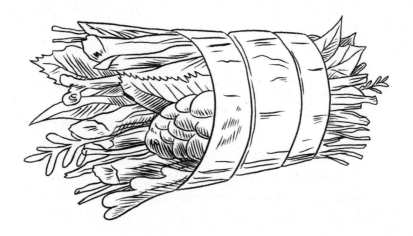

along with supporting mini engineers in practising the basics of design and construction. It's great for developing fine motor skills, learning about insects and understanding the properties of natural materials.

Natural resources needed:

- Hollow bamboo
- Moss
- Small, dry sticks
- Pieces of tree bark
- Straw
- Dry grass
- Dry leaves
- Pebbles/gravel/small stones
- Sand

Also required:

- Plastic bottle or tin cans
- Scissors
- Twine

Optional inspirational read:

- *Bug Hotel* by Libby Walden

1. Building a bug hotel for your balcony, your garden or even to hang out of a bedroom window provides insects and other minibeasts with a safe space to shelter. To prepare for this creation, you need to go out into your

garden or the local park and scavenge for natural materials you can use to create your small bug hotel. Almost anything you can find on a forest floor will work for insects. Think of each different natural material as a different room for the bugs. Some insects will prefer to burrow into the bark, whereas others may crawl inside hollow bamboo canes.

2. You first need to find a container in which to house your mini bug hotel. A cylinder made from an old 2-litre water bottle can be ideal for this as it allows you to see inside your bug hotel. If you'd prefer to make this plastic-free, you can use an old tin can but make sure to remove both ends of the tin first and ensure an adult checks there are no sharp edges.

3. To build your bug hotel, start layering your 'bug rooms' by layering your various natural materials, making sure to not pack too tightly so that plenty of air gets inside.

4. Tie some twine around your bug hotel and have a walk around to identify where you believe your minibeast friends would be happiest located. Some insects like dark areas, whereas other insects like to be in the sun, so choose your mini bug hotel location wisely. Ideally you want it to be located in a place that won't get too rained on and will be sheltered from high winds.

5. Once you've finished with the construction of the interior of your mini bug hotel and think you have rooms for all of your insect friends, either decorate the outside – or do what my children love to do and make beautiful signs to direct the minibeasts to their new palace.

6. Hang your mini bug hotel and try to leave it for at least two weeks to give minibeasts a chance to move in, then take some minibeast safari expeditions to explore your bug hotel and see who has moved in.

Thread and paint leaves (Natural art bunting)

An easy way to make beautiful art and to help your child identify leaves and species of trees and shrubs is to create natural bunting.

Although this bunting won't last for ever, it is free and so can be replaced regularly. It's lovely to try it out with different types of trees throughout the year. You can notice which trees come into leaf during the different seasons and get a deeper understanding of the magic of nature. Try not to strip trees or bushes of too many leaves (it's better to use ones that have fallen from the trees) and do check that you are not disturbing any creatures that may be living on the leaves.

Natural resources needed:

A collection of similar sized leaves (or go crazy and make a collection of your favourite leaves whatever their size). Ensure that all leaves are large enough to be able to be hole punched; ideally they need to be a minimum length of approximately 5 cm (2 in).

Also required:

- ◆ Hole punch
- ◆ Twine
- ◆ Paint and a paintbrush

1. Once you have collected all of your leaves, choose five-ten favourites and lay them on the floor in the order you'd like them to appear on your bunting.

2. Choose your paint colours and paint each leaf front and back then leave to dry.

3. Once the leaves are dry, very gently punch a hole in each of them and thread your twine through to create leaf bunting.

4. Hang up anywhere to make your world brighter.

Hapa zome

Hapa zome printing is a lovely and simple natural dyeing technique that originated in Japan. You can print beautiful creations onto fabric by choosing lush and colourful leaves and flowers and simply pressing out their juices to make a print.

My children and I have made lovely fabric for bunting and gift wrap and simple decorative fabric pieces as gifts. It is an easy and fun way of decorating, with the hammering being a particularly satisfying activity. Children are rarely allowed to use tools, so they love the feeling of trust and being given responsibility.

Natural resources needed:
- Interesting-shaped leaves
- Colourful flowers and petals

Also required:
- White cotton fabric, cut into squares of 15–30 cm (6–12 in)
- Mallet or hammer
- Chopping board, cut side of tree log or flat surface on the ground

1. Your first task for this creation is to go into your garden or the local park and scavenge for beautiful and colourful leaves and flowers.

2. Decide where you are going to hapa zome and set up your area. You will need to spread out your cotton fabric on a flat surface that is OK to be hammered – a log seat, a chopping board or any other flat surface.

3. Carefully spread your cotton fabric until smooth, then take a selection of your leaves and flowers and lay on top to make any pattern your heart desires. Carefully lay a second piece of fabric over the top of your creation, making sure not to move any of the flora underneath.

4. With short, sharp taps, hammer on top of your top sheet and watch as the colours start to bleed and spread through the fabric.

5. When it looks as though most of the colour has bled through your fabric, which depending on the age of your child and the speed of their hammering can take anything from 5–15 minutes, gently remove the top layer of fabric.

6. Hang up your beautiful piece of fabric to dry.

7.   Once the fabric is dry, brush off any excess flowers or leaves that remain and you have a beautifully colourful leaf and flower patterned fabric. Hang it up and display or use as very environmentally friendly reusable gift wrap.

Make a journey stick/wand

Making a journey stick is a really lovely activity and it can be used in so many ways. Sometimes we make them as records of journeys we have made on an adventure walk, other times they are used as walking sticks. Often they can also inspire storytelling.

Natural resources needed:

♦ A stick
♦ Petals, flowers or leaves

Also required:

♦ Twine

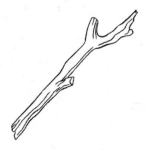

1. First you need to choose a very special stick to be your journey stick or wand. Find one that's at least as thick as your thumb and at least as long as your forearm, ideally one that's fallen to the ground so it's dry.

2. Carefully wrap twine around your stick, leaving space at the bottom for you to hold the stick.

3. Head out on a walk to decorate your stick with flowers, leaves, acorns or anything else that takes your fancy – or use pre-collected materials – securing your natural materials under your twine.

Nature paintbrush

It's really nice when children tap into their creativity and realise that they can be spontaneous without needing to buy stuff. One of the simplest things they can make is a nature paintbrush. It may not give you the precision strokes of a fine artist's brush, but it is free, easily available and invokes a real feeling of pride when you paint with a brush you created.

Natural resources needed:

- ♦ Sticks
- ♦ Petals or flowers, in various shapes, sizes and textures
- ♦ Leaves, in various shapes, sizes and textures

Also required:

- ♦ Elastic bands or twine
- ♦ Paints in various colours
- ♦ Pallet/paint pots
- ♦ Large sheets of paper

Optional inspirational read:

- ♦ *Mix It Up!* by Hervé Tullet

1. Your first task is to find some sturdy sticks, roughly the size of a paintbrush, that can be used as brushes.

2. Wrap the elastic bands around your sticks, or tie twine (wrapped around the stick at least three times) to the tops of your sticks.

3. Head out for a walk and select five to six different natural materials that you believe would make good tips for your paintbrushes, or use pre-collected materials.

4. Carefully slide the stems of the leaves/flowers etc. into your elastic band or twine until it's securely attached to your stick.

5. Pour out some paints into paint pots or pallets. Using your newly made paint brushes, experiment with different textures and colours on paper. Which is your favourite paintbrush and why?

Puddle jumping

This one needs no resources or instructions, other than: wear your most waterproof wellies, tuck your waterproof trousers into your boots, go find the biggest puddles you can find – and start jumping!

Rock sculptures/towers

There is an amazing artist called Andy Goldsworthy who makes incredible art out of natural materials. My children and I love looking at his work and it often inspires us to create something beautiful from things that don't seem particularly amazing on their own.

Natural resources needed:
♦ Rocks or pebbles, as flat as you can find

Optional resources:
♦ Coloured sticks of chalk

Optional inspirational read:
♦ *Andy Goldsworthy: A Collaboration with Nature*

1. Before you start you need to find some inspiration for beautiful rock sculptures. I'd recommend taking a look at some Andy Goldsworthy sculptures before heading out to find some suitable materials. If you don't have the book, or even if you do, for more inspiration go online and look up Andy Goldsworthy's beautiful art.

2. Collect a number of rocks or pebbles and let your
    creativity flow. Will you build a rock tower? A rock
    spiral? Or will you create rock animals?

3. To add some extra colour and another dimension to your
    rock art, consider adding some colour using chalk. It'll
    wash off the rocks the next time it rains.

Clay animals

Working with clay is multi-sensory and therapeutic. It also builds both gross and fine motor skills, including the small muscles in hands and fingers which are used for hand-writing.

I've suggested making these as after being lucky enough to see some real hedgehogs crawling around our garden we went through a bit of a clay-hedgehog making phase. But this activity can be adapted using the same resources for whatever animals your children would like to make.

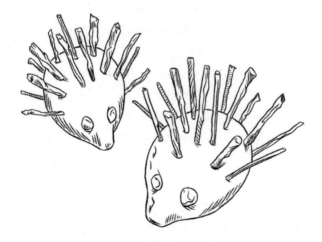

Natural resources needed:
- Small twigs
- Acorns and small stones
- Air-drying clay, or mud

Optional inspirational reads:

- *The Hodgeheg* by Dick King-Smith
- *Hedgehogs Don't Live in the City!* by Lucy Reynolds and Jenna Herman

1. Your first task is to find some small twigs for the hedgehog spikes. You are aiming to have all of your spikes more or less the same size, so try snapping your twigs until you have a variety of similar-length hedgehog quills.

2. Next, make the hedgehog's body. Taking a ball of clay in your hand, manipulate it until it is an oval shape. When you've achieved the shape, start to pull out one end of the clay to a point to form the hedgehog's snout.

3. Once you have your hedgehog's body and face shape ready, start adding some detail such as eyes, nostrils and a mouth. You can use a stick as a tool to carve these in or, for example, add some small stones or acorns to make the eyes.

4. All your hedgehog needs now are quills. Start pushing twigs from your pile into the clay at an angle to form the spikes.

5. Leave your hedgehog to air-dry and firm up. You could even build him a hedgehog home while you are waiting for him to dry?

Build a dam

Playing with water is a magical experience. It's often easy to forget how amazing water is: it flows downhill, it can continually change shape, and every living thing on earth needs it to survive!

Humans have attempted to harness water for thousands of years. Become part of this journey by making your own little dam or river. Children adore playing with water. It stimulates all of their senses, is enormous fun and, with this particular activity, challenges you to think critically and problem-solve.

Natural resources needed:

- Sticks, stones, bark, moss, anything natural and bulky
- A large puddle or flowing water!

1. You first need to find some water you can safely play with. Be it a large puddle or some flowing water, sit and observe the water for a while. Have a think about how you could change the flow of the water. Do you want to split one puddle into two? Or do you want to alter the direction of water flow in a stream?

2. Once you've decided upon your mission, start collecting materials to build a dam.

3. Carefully start placing your sticks, stones and other natural materials to block one area of water off. Did you succeed? If not, why not? What can you do differently? How can you experiment to achieve different results?

Make rafts and float them

From their earliest days, my children loved local streams and ponds. Whenever we came upon water, like most children, they were instantly attracted to it. Depending on the depth, we often paddle, exploring the water through immersion in it. On days when I want us to keep dry but still want to encourage that fascination and love of water play, we explore and hypothesise with floating and sinking. What materials float, which sink? Let's make our predictions and then throw our objects in to observe what happens!

Once this play has reached its limit, we move on to building rafts, which have become ever more elaborate as our children have grown. We've even created rafts that were big enough to float our enthusiastic pets on!

Natural resources needed:
♦ Sticks and bark
♦ A stream/river/large puddle/pond/paddling pool/bath

Also required:
♦ Twine
♦ Paper to make sails
♦ Glue
♦ Scissors
♦ Sharpies or pencils to decorate your sail

Optional inspirational read:
♦ *The Real Boat* by Marina Aromshtam
♦ *The Explorer* by Katherine Rundell (for older children but a brilliant read-aloud book)

1. Your first task is to collect some materials to use to build your raft. You are looking for dry sticks, bark or twigs – lots of them.

2. When you've collected your materials, have a think about what size raft you would like to create. Lay out your sticks and let your child talk you through their

ideas of how they could build a raft that will float – this is a great critical-thinking and problem-solving activity!

3. It's likely your child will have some fantastic ideas on how to make their raft, so let them experiment. The technique we use is to tie a clove hitch knot to start us off (there are some great YouTube video tutorials on this), then we weave our twine under and over one way to bind our sticks, and then back the other way with the opposite under-over pattern. Depending on how large your raft is, you may then need some sticks to be attached going in the opposite direction to stabilise it.

4. If you'd like to make a sail, choose a suitable stick to act as a mast and cut out a sail from paper. Decorate it as colourfully as you like. Attach your mast to the raft and then glue on your sail and you are ready to test out your raft!

5. Carefully carry your raft to the water and gently place it on the surface. Does it float or does it sink? If it sinks, why? What can you do to improve your design? If it floats, hurray! Hours of fun can now be had as you experiment with how fast your raft can travel in the water and what objects are light enough to be cargo on your raft. So many opportunities for experimentation and play.

Build a nest

My children love nests. They make nests in the garden to try and tempt birds to lay eggs, and they make their own nests for us to snuggle up in and read a book or role play mummy and baby birds. Nests are lovely warm, cosy spaces and come in a huge variety of shapes and sizes.

Natural resources needed:

- Sticks
- Twigs
- Bark
- Grass
- Dried leaves
- Feathers
- Moss

Optional inspirational reads:

- *Bird House* (A Clover Robin Book of Nature) by Libby Walden and Clover Robin
- *Bird Builds a Nest* by Martin Jenkins

1. Start by collecting some materials to use to build your nest. You are looking for any kind of nest-building materials. Think about bird nests you've spotted in the

past. What have they looked like? What shape have they been? What have they been made from?

2. Decide where you'd like to locate your nest. How big do you want it to be? Some children like to make nests for small birds, others like to make nests big enough for them to fit inside!

3. Start to layer your sticks and twigs to form your circular nest. Build up the structure of your wall until you have achieved the size and shape you desire. If you'd like to, you can add more stability to your structure by adding mud between the layers.

4. Once your base structure is complete, it's time to decorate your nest with your scavenged natural materials. Then hop inside or role play to your heart's content!

Build a fairy home and garden

There is something lovely about the idea of fairies living in a tiny corner of your garden. It's even lovelier to tap into this mystery with your children, helping them to create their own secret spaces.

How you develop your fairy garden depends on your child. My children loved to paint some natural materials and enhance the garden with new materials as they found them through the week, often morphing their design from a fairy garden to a dinosaur world or animal kingdom. A friend of mine used to have a fairy who left letters for her daughter in her fairy spot, which her daughter then used to reply to. How gorgeous!

Optional natural resources:

- Sticks
- Logs to create shapes
- Twigs
- Bark
- Acorn caps
- Pinecones
- Flowers or petals
- Pebbles
- Moss

Optional other resources:

- Fabric pieces
- Lollipop sticks
- Paint and paintbrushes
- Hot glue gun
- Cardboard cereal box or empty tin can (ensure there are no sharp edges)

Optional inspirational read:

- *Aziza's Secret Fairy Door* by Lola Morayo

1. Before you start creating, collect some materials to use to build your fairy house. If you want to start with a solid structure, use a tin can or an old cereal box to form the base of your fairy house. We usually start with building a one-room house/shelter for our fairy.

2. Either using sticks to construct a house or your tin can/ cardboard box, design and glue or balance together your components until you have a 'room'.

3. Then comes the fun part: decorate your fairy house. Use bark, flowers, moss, pieces of old fabric or anything your heart desires.

4. Once your fairy house is complete, you can move on to creating a fairy garden outside the house. Use pebbles to form the paths in your garden, between your moss, flowers or any other decorative flourishes.

5. If you have the patience and time, do as my children love doing and snap twigs into tiny pieces and glue them together to make tiny chairs and tables. Acorn cups make perfect tiny bowls or cups for tea parties.

6. A final flourish and easy to build is a twig fence around your fairy home and garden. Do this by pushing twigs into the mud in a line around the perimeter of the garden.

Grow something from seed

Growing a plant from a tiny seed is one of the most incredible gifts that nature can give us. And it is something so easy that anyone can do it.

You first need to decide what you would like to grow. Flowers are beautiful and rewarding but the joy of children being able to eventually eat something they have planted and lovingly tended from a seed is a powerful lesson in where food comes from ... and is incredibly rewarding. If you do choose to grow fruit or vegetables, you may find your child is willing to

be more adventurous with their eating. Always try to buy your
seeds from a British company – it means less air miles and
also that your seeds will be suited for the British climate.

Natural resources needed:

- Soil
- Seeds
- Compost

Also required:

- Lollipop sticks
- Sharpie pen
- Biodegradable planting pots or egg cartons or
  repurposed pots from other plants
- Small watering can

Recommended first seeds:

- Tomatoes
- Peas
- Cucumbers
- Lettuce
- Pumpkins
- Sunflowers
- Nasturtiums

Optional inspirational reads:

- *Seed to Plant* (National Georgraphic Kids) by Kristin
  Baird Rattini
- *Errol's Garden* by Gillian Hibbs

♦ POT GANG subscription highly recommended, although expensive

1. Place some compost in your chosen pots and water the soil gently to moisten it.

2. Get out your lollipop sticks and label them by writing or drawing the names of your seeds so you remember which are which.

3. After reading the seed packet for instructions, plant your seeds gently in your chosen pots (this is a fabulous fine motor-skills activity) and cover with soil. The majority of seeds like to be covered by a layer of soil, but some need light to germinate and will want to rest on top of the prepared soil.

4. Water very gently as you don't want to wash the seeds around the pot.

5. Ensuring you don't over-water during the next growth phase, keep the soil damp and nurture your seeds into seedlings. If too many seedlings appear and are overcrowding your container, thin out the seedlings by gently moving some of them to another pot (see step 6).

6. Before moving your seedlings to their new home – either another, larger pot or straight into a garden bed, we need to prepare the new environment. Fill with soil/compost

and use a pencil or a straw to push a hole into the soil. Use a teaspoon to help loosen seedlings from their pot, but if you can manage this with your hands, go ahead. Be very gentle when removing the seedlings as this is a delicate stage and they can be easily damaged.

7. Pop your seedlings into the soil; ideally you want their lower leaves touching the top of the soil, so plant as far down as you can. Any remaining seedlings in their original pot can be planted straight into the ground or into a larger pot.

8. Continue to nurture your seedlings and look forward to harvesting your first crop.

Minibeast hunt

If you have children anything like mine, this activity will occupy them for hours and can expand into building homes (see page 38) for their new minibeast friends. Minibeasts – invertebrates (small animals without a backbone), like a spider, snail, beetle, centipede or worm – are everywhere (like it or not!) and whether you are looking at their faces up close or the way they move around the garden, they are a source of fascination. My children have always loved them, particularly beetles, woodlice, caterpillars, moths and butterflies.

Natural resources needed:

+ None!

Optional resources:

+ Magnifying glass
+ Small paintbrush
+ Jar or bug container
+ Minibeast ID book (Woodland Trust do a brilliant portable book)

Optional inspirational reads:

+ *Mad about Minibeasts!* by Giles Andreas
+ DK First Facts: *Bugs*

1. Minibeasts often like dark places in the garden or in the forest, so you need to be very observant and go on a small animal hunt! Lift up logs or stones to see what's hiding underneath. Look closely at the bark of fallen trees or logs as minibeasts love dead wood. Little eyes seem to be far better at spotting these tiny creatures than adult eyes.

2. When you do spot some minibeasts, sit and watch them for a while. What do you think they're doing?

3. If you have a minibeast ID book, can you identify the minibeast? If you have the equipment and you'd like to take a closer look, using your paintbrush gently pick up the minibeast and pop it into a jar. Examine your

find carefully, look at the detail of its incredible body through your magnifying glass.

4. Always try to put your minibeasts carefully back where you found them when you've finished exploring and investigating.

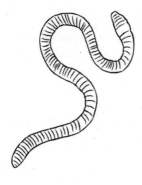

Make a nature bracelet

One of the ways that my youngest daughter manages the difficult balance of being a bit of a fashionista while also a wild child is to make beautiful accessories out of natural materials. I often spot her in the garden or local park collecting colourful leaves or flowers, and then a day or two later she emerges adorned with some wonderful arrangement of nature.

Natural resources needed:

- Flowers
- Acorns
- Leaves
- Sticks
- Grass
- Feathers

Also required:

- Double-sided sticky tape
- Cardboard
- Scissors

Optional inspirational read:

- *The Tiny Seed* by Eric Carle

1. Cut a strip of card to be your bracelet. You want it loose enough that you will be able to take it off at the end of the day but not so loose that it falls off.

2. Once you have your desired length of card, using your sticky tape join each end together.

3. Here's the fiddly part! Tape double-sided sticky tape to cover your bracelet entirely. Then, when your bracelet is covered, you will need to peel off the exposed backing of the tape so that your bracelet is now sticky and ready for decorating.

4. If you haven't collected already, take a walk through nature and pick up any beautiful natural resources you see which you think would make a lovely decoration for your bracelet. Push them firmly onto your bracelet to cover up the sticky tape completely.

5. Once your bracelet is complete, wear it with pride!

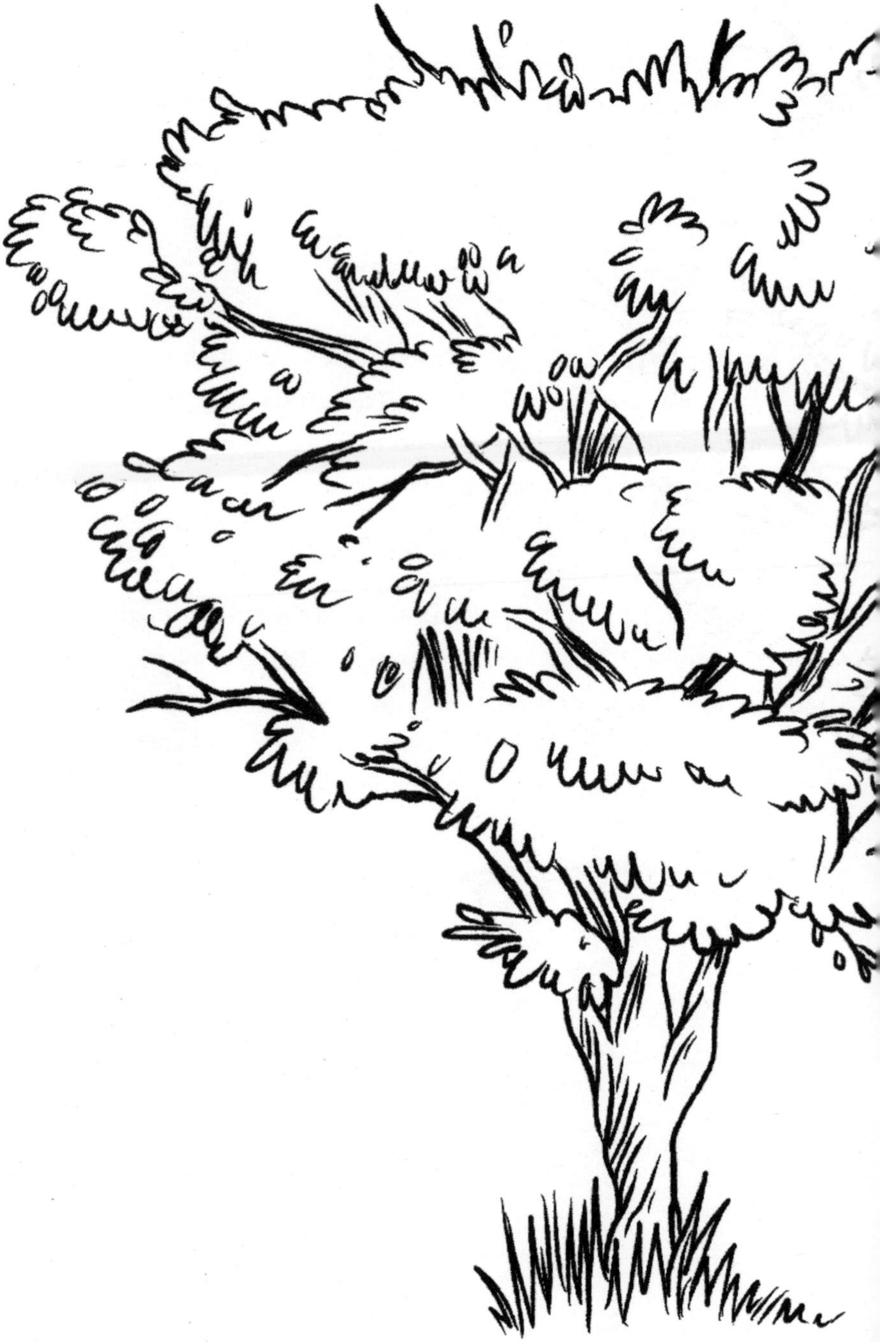

4.

Activities for Summer

Make a potion

Potion-making is an activity that will fascinate children of all ages and it can be as simple or intricately detailed as you would like. There is something so magical about mixing different concoctions and seeing what will happen! These potions can be used to create magic spells or anything else that captures your child's imagination (but please make sure not to drink them).

Natural resources needed:

+ Flowers, grass, leaves

Also required:

+ Water
+ Bowls, bottles, measuring cups, measuring spoons, water, pipettes

Optional resources:

+ Pestle and mortar, food colouring, herbs, spices, labels and coloured pencils, empty clean spice jars/ mini bottles

Optional inspirational reads:

+ *George's Marvellous Medicine* by Roald Dahl
+ *Stone Soup* by Jess Stockham
+ *Encyclopedia of Herbal Medicine* by DK Natural Health

1. Start by using a pestle and mortar or two stones to grind up some petals, grasses or other natural materials so that the natural dyes and fragrance of the materials are released.

2. Once you have all of the materials in front of you, mix up the natural materials and their dyes in various sensory combinations, using your hands or a wooden

spoon and experimenting with texture and smell. This isn't an activity that needs much adult intervention as once you have set up all of the resources; the best thing you can do is step back and allow deep exploration to take place.

3. For older children, this activity can easily be extended into creating herbal remedies. My own children are happy to spend hours on end creating and developing these. It's great if they can research the medicinal properties of common garden plants and combine them to create lovely potions.

Make a magic wand

Many children have been swept up in the Harry Potter craze in the past few years. Mine were no exception! Making your own magic wand is a lovely thing to do at home – and will save you a fortune!

Natural resources needed:
- A stick
- Petals or flowers
- Leaves

Also required:
- Strips of fabric
- Craft wire or string

Optional inspirational read:
- Any of the Harry Potter books by J. K. Rowling

1. Find a stick the right length to be a wand, with a good thickness so you can hold the wand easily but sturdy enough to decorate.

2. Tie one end of your string or wire securely to the bottom end of the stick and start wrapping it around at an angle,

creating diagonal loops up and around your magic wand. When you reach the top, wind the loops closer together.

3.   Take your strips of fabric and tuck them into the top loops of the wire or string. Vary both size and colour as this will form the colourful top of your wand.

4.   Using petals, flowers or leaves, decorate the remainder of your wand by sliding your petals and leaves in a decorative pattern between the wire/string and your stick.

5.   Once you have completed your decoration, let your imagination inspire you and make some magic!

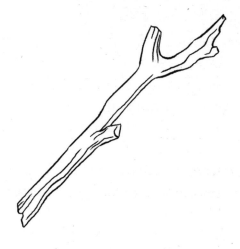

Make a nature crown

A particularly easy activity for a birthday party, making nature crowns is fun. It's a great activity to do with a group of friends and feels very special.

Natural resources needed:
  ♦ Leaves, petals, twigs, pine cones, acorns, grasses

Also required:
  ♦ Cardboard
  ♦ Double-sided sticky tape or hot glue gun
  ♦ Scissors

Optional inspirational read:

♦ *The Crown on your Head* by Nancy Tillman

1. Measure and cut a length of cardboard that will fit around your child's head and form a circular base for your crown. Seal at each end with sticky tape. Go for a good fit as too loose a crown may slide down once the weight of your 'jewels' are added.

2. Take a look at the size and colour of your crown, then gather natural resources that you think are worthy of it. Lay them all out so you have a draft of placement before you start sticking your decorations on; it's always good to review your design before you commit.

3. Once you have the placement design of your decorations, either start using a hot glue gun to start sticking the decorations onto your cardboard crown, or attach double-sided sticky tape to the outside of your crown and then peel off the backing tape before starting to stick your decorations onto it.

4. When you've finished, wear your crown with pride!

Dye a T-shirt with natural dyes

There's something amazing about using natural dyes to make a plain white T-shirt colourful. And the colours that can emerge from common fruits and vegetables are astounding! The results won't last as long as traditional dyes, which of course you can substitute for the natural dyes, but there's something so satisfying and wholesome about making your own natural dyes – it feels almost old fashioned. I recommend starting with one or two colours to begin with.

Natural resources needed:

- ◆ A selection of brightly coloured plants, fruit or vegetables, such as:
  - o Red cabbage
  - o Green leaves (spinach, nettles or mint are good choices)
  - o Beetroot
  - o Blackberries
  - o Blueberries
  - o Turmeric

Also required:

- Knife
- Peeler
- Chopping board
- Saucepans (one for each colour)
- Water
- Strainer
- Stainless steel bowls/glass jars
- White T-shirts
- Elastic bands

Optional resources:

- Newspapers and gloves to protect your surfaces and hands

1. Once you have chosen your selected natural resources, chop and peel (if necessary) your plants/vegetables/ fruits. Put each coloured plant into a separate saucepan, cover with water and simmer each for at least two hours to bring out the natural dyes. If you can prep the night before and simmer them for a few hours, the dye will be a richer colour.

2. Remove from the heat and allow to cool. Strain out the plant/vegetable/fruit and pour the resulting dyes into stainless-steel bowls or glass jars – or another container you don't mind getting stained! – one for each colour.

3. Meanwhile, prep your white T-shirt by washing it first. Once it's clean, simmer the T-shirt in 4 parts water and 1 part vinegar for one hour, then rinse clean with cold water.

4. Keeping your T-shirt damp, randomly gather up bunches of fabric and twist then secure with elastic bands into lots of little knots – the more random the better.

5. On a first attempt, I would recommend one or two colours to be used per T-shirt. Gathering your T-shirt into sections, drop either the entire T-shirt or each half of the T-shirt into the bowl or glass jar of dye. Let the T-shirt soak for at least one hour. If you can leave it overnight it will have a more potent dye colour.

6. Once the T-shirt has soaked for one hour, and before removing the elastic bands, rinse the T-shirt thoroughly.

7. Remove the elastic bands and hang your unique custom-made T-shirt up to dry.

Build a pond

Ponds are amazing habitats for all kinds of wildlife. It only takes a few minutes of careful observation to find a myriad of creatures that you would normally never notice.

The great thing about making a pond is that it doesn't have to be enormous. Even a small pond will attract water creatures over time. I often find my Tupperware has been commandeered for tiny pond making, but can't help but smile at the love my children have for trying to improve biodiversity. I keep an eye on mini ponds and retrieve my containers within a couple of weeks if the pond dries up.

The first thing to do is to take a walk around your garden, or take a look at your balcony and try to work out where you would like your pond to be located. It would be nice if it received some sunlight during parts of the day but your pond shouldn't be in direct sunlight all day.

Natural resources needed:

♦ Sticks
♦ Rocks
♦ Pond plants

Also required:

♦ Spade
♦ Watertight container (a plastic washing up bowl, Tupperware container or similar)

Optional inspirational reads:

♦ *Tad* by Benji Davies
♦ *First Book of Pond Life* (RSPB) by Derek Niemann

1. Dig a hole large enough to bury your container (pond) or if you don't want to dig a hole, choose a nice location to place your container on.

2. Add a layer of rocks to the bottom and build a rock or stick staircase out of your pond in case any creatures

fall in and need to climb back out. (Once some of our school students built a lovely ramp out of sticks with raised bars as they were worried about hedgehogs falling into the pond they restored. It's remained one of my favourite parts of our school grounds.)

3.   Leave your container outside to collect rainwater. You don't want to use tap water for a wildlife pond as it contains chemicals.

4.   While you're waiting for your pond to fill with rainwater, take a trip to a garden centre and buy some pond plants. In asking the opinion of the five-year-old children who restored our school pond, they say the best pond plants are Lesser Spearwort, Hornwort and Waterlilies.

5.   As your pond fills with rainwater, watch and wait. I wonder which creatures will come along to explore your pond?

Fairy wings

Children love to role play. Adding costumes and props can often extend the activity. And what better a prop than one they've made themselves.

Natural resources needed:
+ 4 bendy young sticks (young hazel or willow will be nice and malleable)
+ Flowers, leaves, grasses

Also required:
+ Craft wire or string
+ Elastic cord (or can be substituted for more string)

1. Your first task is to find some suitable sticks to form the structure of your fairy wings and then collect some beautiful natural materials to decorate them with. You are going to be threading your decorations onto your wings, so aim to collect items with decent-length stems.

2. Choose two larger sticks and two smaller sticks and lay them on the ground.

3. Take the two larger sticks and bend them to join at either end, making a fairy wing shape. Wrap your string or craft wire repeatedly around the two ends, ensuring they are joined securely. Repeat with the smaller sticks.

4. Once all four sticks have been bent into shape, place them on the ground with the two larger wings on top and the two smaller wings below. Using craft wire or string, tie the top two wings together, and the bottom two wings together, before joining the top wings to the bottom wings. You will need to weave your string around and through the wings several times to get this really secure, so if you have coloured string, why not make this into a feature of your wings?

5. When your wings are securely attached, wind string across each wing to make a grid-like pattern. Taking your flowers, leaves and grasses, weave them into the string to decorate your beautiful fairy wings.

6. Measure out two loops of elastic cord (or more string) that will hold your wings securely on your child's shoulders. Tie the elastic loops onto the wings, securely attaching the elastic as best you can as this is the part that will be most pulled on.

Mud kitchen

A mud kitchen can be as simple or elaborate as you like. Either way, children will adore the opportunity to mix, create and role play in a sensory kitchen where mud, water and natural materials are the main ingredients. The beauty of mud kitchen play is that it allows for really deep sensory, messy play, as well as offering endless opportunities for social interactions.

Resources needed:

- Old kitchen equipment (charity shops are great for this) – saucepans, kitchen utensils, wooden spoons, measuring spoons, measuring jugs, measuring cups, stainless steel mixing bowls
- Watering can

Optional resources:

- To enhance your mud kitchen, try using:
  - Scavenged building materials such as pallets, old cupboards, shelves to build a 'hob' or 'oven'
  - Hooks to hang your kitchen utensils on
  - Plastic jars to store your ingredients in
  - Chalkboard and chalk for writing recipes, cafe signs, or whatever suits your role play
  - Ice-cream scooper
  - Whisk
  - Sieve
  - Pestle and mortar
  - Potato masher
  - Funnels
  - Weighing scales
  - Muffin trays or silicone cupcake cases for your little treasures
  - Teapots
  - Enamel mugs

Optional inspirational read:

- *Stone Soup* by Jess Stockham

1.   Start by building or choosing where to site your play kitchen. A mud kitchen can be as simple as an area of soil that's able to be dug, along with spoons and some pots and pans. Anything else you manage to scavenge can always be added later. It's worth setting up a mud kitchen as best you can as children will spend hours of creative play in it.

2.   You are aiming to set up an area that allows your child to experiment with recipes. There are countless mud kitchen recipe books you can buy, but I can almost guarantee that none of the ideas they have for mud kitchen concoctions will be as great as your children's. Start off their mud kitchen baking journey by asking them to make you a hot chocolate, or a birthday cake. Once they've made their first treat for you, you'll have hours of enjoying mud kitchen treats ahead of you.

Cloud spotting

It's often the simplest things that are the best and we can
forget the magic of the sky above us. Take some time to relax
with your child – lie back and watch the sky unfold. Have
a chat about what you see, you will be amazed where your
imagination can take you.

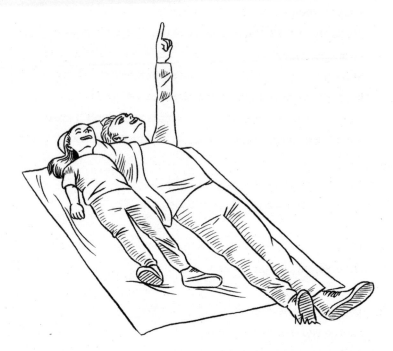

Resources needed:

- A comfortable space to lie, or a picnic blanket to lie on
- Paper and pencils/chalk
- Sunglasses if it's a bright day

Optional inspirational read:

- *Clouds* (National Geographic Kids: Explore My World) by Marfe Ferguson Delano

1. Find a comfortable place, lie yourself down and take a moment to watch the clouds pass by. This can be a very relaxing activity as well as provoking your imagination and offering opportunities for scientific learning. Make sure you never look directly at the sun.

2. What can you see? Can you spot any animal shapes hiding in the clouds? What do you think the cloud animals are doing? Can you make up a story about the cloud animals?

3. How fast are the clouds moving across the sky? Does their shape change as they move?

4. What types of clouds can you see? Would you like to sketch the clouds to remember the types you have seen and try to identify them?

5.   The most common clouds you are likely to see are:

Cirrus clouds are thin and wispy. They are most likely to be seen in good weather.

Cumulus clouds are rounded and puffy – they are what you draw when you are asked to draw a cloud. You will usually see these on sunny days.

Stratocumulus clouds are the clouds you see most often in the UK. They are uniform and flat, can be white or grey and are mostly seen with drizzly weather and on days where cloud cover blocks out the sun.

Bird-watching

No matter where you go on Earth, you will find some kind of bird. Big ones, little ones, hopefully both! It's an activity that you can take anywhere with you, and developing a love and appreciation of birds is something that children can take with them their whole lives.

Resources needed:
- Binoculars
- Bird ID book
- Camera (optional)
- Paper and pencils
- Patience, lots of it!

Optional inspirational reads:
- *Shh! We Have a Plan* by Chris Haughton
- *Starbird* by Sharon King-Chai
- *The Big Book of Birds* (National Geographic Kids) by Yuval Zommer
- *First Book of Birds* (RSPB) by Anita Ganeri and David Chandler
- *The Little Book of Garden Bird Songs* by Caz Buckingham and Andrea Pinnington

1. For your first time bird-watching, decide if you'd like
    to give yourself a challenge. If so, the RSPB website has
    some brilliant bird-watching activity sheets.

2. Aim for somewhere you'll be able to sit still for a while.
    Take a snack and a drink and take some time to sit and
    just listen. See if you can recognise any of the bird songs
    you know and identify birds that way.

3. The quieter you manage to be when you sit, the more
    relaxed the birds will become around you and the closer
    they will approach. Take a look at the birds you see and
    use your binoculars to spot more details.

4. Examine the colour, the shape, the size and the beak of
    the birds and try to identify them. Ask your child some
    wondering questions: I wonder what each bird you see
    likes to eat? I wonder where they might nest? Why don't
    you draw your favourite birds and take your drawings
    home to display?

Tree climbing

Climbing a tree is such a natural pleasure, simultaneously stimulating your senses while calming you. Children and adults of all ages enjoy this activity, but maybe it's been a while since you tried it? It's a great activity for children to engage in to learn to feel comfortable with a little bit of (safe) fear and to start to gain the knowledge of self-risk assessments and management.

Children may sense that tree climbing is something exciting and so feel trusted by adults to be able to engage in this activity. A challenging rule for adults is to resist the urge to help. For even the two-year-olds in our forest nurseries, our rule for tree climbing was always: 'I can help you with my words but not my hands.' A child must be encouraged to climb unaided. If they climb up, they are very likely to be able to climb down safely, whereas a child who has been boosted or lifted to a height they couldn't achieve themselves might then find themselves in a dangerous situation when it's time to climb down.

Resources needed:

- ♦ A sturdy tree
- ♦ Flexible shoes with good grip
- ♦ No loose jewellery
- ♦ Clothes you can really move in

Optional inspirational read (for both parents and children!):

- ♦ *Mama Miti: Wangari Maathai and the Trees of Kenya* by Donna Jo Napoli

1. The first rule of tree climbing is to check for loose branches and that the tree is safe. Do not climb trees in the rain or if they are wet as the trunk and branches can get slippery.

2. Start low and slow. You and your child will build confidence as you climb.

3. Marvel at your child's climbing achievements and if you are concerned about their climbing, be sure not to use the phrase 'Be careful'. This sends a message to them that what they are doing is dangerous, which could make their movements more hesitant, less confident and therefore more dangerous. To offer support instead be specific, short and positive with your advice.

Blackberry picking and painting

One of my favourite summer activities is to go blackberry picking with my children. We take some stainless steel or plastic food containers or a bucket, head out into our local nature reserve or along the pavement near our home where there are blackberries growing along the side of the road and we pick until we can't pick any more. I make sure on these days not to wear anything I mind getting stained!

When we decide we have finished blackberry picking and are victorious with our haul, it's time to decide what we will do with our bounty. Depending on how many we've collected, we will either wash and eat them straight away or turn them into a blackberry crumble or blackberry jam. Once we've eaten our fill, we love to use what we have leftover to make blackberry paint.

Resources needed:

- Plastic or stainless steel containers or buckets
- Blackberries
- Paper and paintbrushes
- Pestle and mortar or two rocks

1. Collect as many blackberries as you are able. Choose the juicy ones that almost fall off the stems. Just make sure they are high enough and out of the way from areas any dogs may have been visiting!

2. This is an activity which most certainly belongs outside as it's very messy, but it's very sensory and good fun. Depending on what we have available, we either use a pestle and mortar to squish the blackberries, or a rock to squash the blackberries into their container. At times when we have nothing else, we use our hands to squeeze and squelch all of the blackberries until they release their juices and are mushy.

3. Once you have your blackberry paint you can dip a paintbrush into it and paint beautiful vibrant colours on paper. If you want to thicken up your paint to use for creating leaf stencils or the like, stir in a little bit of mud; this will also dilute the colour slightly. We have been known to use it as face paint as well, which can be alarming for passers-by but is brilliant fun!

Fun with dandelions – secret spies and dandelion art

This is an opportunity to be a secret spy on a mission. Dandelions have a secret superpower as they contain a sap that can be used as invisible ink.

Natural resources needed:

♦ Dandelions (don't pick until you're ready to use them!)

Also required:

♦ Paper or card
♦ Scissors

Optional resources:

♦ Double-sided sticky tape

1. Have a think about what invisible drawing, words or message you want to send to someone. When you're ready, snip your dandelion with scissors and, using the stem like a pen, start mark-making on the paper or card. If you have a longer message you may need to continue to trim the stem to reach more sap if it starts to run out.

2. When you've finished writing your secret message, your recipient will need to leave the card or paper out in the sun to dry in order to reveal the hidden message.

3. If you're using a dandelion clock rather than a dandelion flower, try extending your fun by using it for another activity. Using double-sided sticky tape, tape out a shape on your card then peel back the tape backing. Hold up the dandelion clock in front of your sticky tape and give a big blow! How much of your sticky tape is now covered in dandelion seeds? Do you need to find another dandelion to finish off your piece of art?

Shadow art

On sunny days there are many options for beautiful shadow art. It's always amazing to see the different shadows that are created by unusual shapes and objects.

Resources needed:

- Paper
- Coloured pencils or felt-tip pens
- Chalk
- Interesting shaped objects
- String and pegs
- Sunshine!

OPTION 1: CHALK SHADOW ART

1. If near your home you have a piece of pavement or paving stones that you can chalk onto, this may be the activity for you.

2. Take a look at the shadows that are being cast onto the pavement or paving stones. Are there any leaves or trees casting an interesting shape? If not, think about how you can position an interesting object, or a toy from home, to cast an interesting shadow.

3. Once you have decided upon a shape that interests you, use your chalk to draw over the shadow on the ground. Make sure you're looking at the shadow and not trying to draw the actual object. Start with the outline of the shadow and then start filling in. Was it a bright sunny day and so your shadow art is crisp and clear? Or was it a cloudier day which meant your shadow art has more blurry lines?

OPTION 2: PENCIL AND PAPER SHADOW ART

1. Lay out a large sheet of paper.

2. Find some toys with interesting shapes (my children always enjoyed doing this with toy animals or dinosaurs).

3. Look at where the sun is falling and set up your toys
    along the edge of the paper so that the shadows fall onto
    the paper.

4. Move around to the other side of the paper so your
    shadow doesn't block out your toy's shadow and start
    to draw round the outline of your shadows. When my
    children engaged in this activity, rather than fill in the
    shadows immediately, we tended to carefully draw the
    outline and then leave the toys in position for a few
    hours to observe how the shadows move and change
    across the paper before colouring in.

Make perfume

Everyone loves a pleasant-smelling fragrance and what better way to make one than by using natural ingredients from your garden or local park? These make lovely gifts for very lucky family and friends.

You can use the scents of your choice. There are some plants and herbs that have a stronger smell, such as rose, jasmine, lilac, honeysuckle and lavender. Mint, rosemary and lemon verbena are great too. My children have also enjoyed this activity many times using daisies, dandelions and anything they can find in the garden, so don't feel you have to have specific ingredients to make this work. As always, it's the process that matters, not the end product.

Natural resources needed:
- Flowers or herbs of your choice

Also required:
- Glass bottles or jars
- Small perfume bottles (if you have them)
- Labels (or sticky tape and paper)
- Pencils or felt-tip pens
- Funnel (make one out of paper if you don't have one)
- Water
- Pestle and mortar (if you have one)

1. Choose the scents you think would work well together. What do you want in your perfume?

2. When you've decided upon your ingredients, pop them one at a time into your pestle and mortar, or if you don't have one find a couple of nice big rocks. For your perfume to smell as strong as possible, you need to crush the flowers or herbs to release the fragrant oils.

3. Using a funnel, decant the crushed flowers, herbs and oils into your perfume bottle or glass jar and top up with water.

4. Leave your perfume for a few hours, or ideally overnight to allow the oils, petals and herbs to really infuse into the water.

5. While your perfume is infusing, why not come up with some interesting names for your perfume? You could also create personalised labels for your perfume by drawing or writing these on pieces of paper or sticky labels. Then decant into small perfume bottles, if you have, and gift away to lucky family members or friends – or simply enjoy yourself.

Sun-prints on print paper

This is a lovely way to make natural prints using some simple processing. It's a good way to keep kids busy and also a gentle introduction to processing techniques that could lead to other hobbies such as photography.

Natural resources needed:

- A sunny day
- Flat, interesting-shaped objects (we love using distinctive leaves)

Also required:

- Sun-print paper
- An old packaging box, big enough to place your sun-print paper on top of
- A waterproof container big enough to hold your sun-print paper
- Water

1. Make sure you have everything ready that you may need and go find your sunny spot to develop your print – ideally where buildings, trees or other fixed objects aren't casting a shadow. You'll also need a shaded area near to your sunny spot where you can set up your print ready to be developed.

2. Set your box in the shaded area. Remove a sheet of the sun-print paper from the packet and place it blue-side up on top of your box.

3. Arrange your interesting objects on top of the sun-print paper quickly, trying not to move them once they are placed. You can pin these down if needed but this will leave holes in your sun-print paper.

4. Once the objects are arranged, move the whole box, sun-print paper and interesting objects into the direct sunlight and leave until the blue starts to fade to pale blue. This takes approximately five minutes.

5. While you are waiting, fill your container with water and place it in the shaded area.

6. Once the sun-print paper has turned pale blue, or five minutes have passed, quickly remove your objects. Take your sun-print paper in your hands by the edges, then submerge it in the container of water, holding it there for at least one minute.

7. Take your sun-print paper out of the water and dry it flat (weighing it down on the corners if needed). Take a look at your amazing sun-print work of art!

5.

Activities for Autumn

Make god's eyes

A god's eye is a beautiful, spiritual object made by weaving coloured wool around a cross formed from wooden sticks. They are commonly found in Mexico and are a really relaxing decoration to make. They will also brighten up your world beautifully.

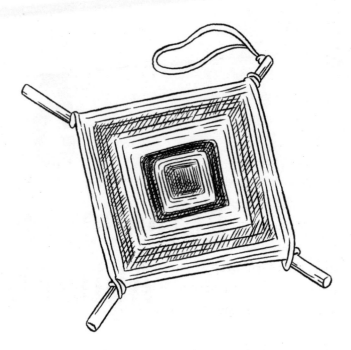

Resources needed:

♦ Two small sticks
♦ Balls of colourful wool

Optional inspirational read:

♦ *Atlas of Adventures* by Rachel Williams

1. To begin, cross your two sticks to make an 'X'.

2. Take the first colour of wool you would like to have at the centre of your decoration, tie a knot to attach it to the first stick and then start wrapping your sticks to give a stable base. Ideally wrap at least a few times in one direction, then turn the sticks and wrap the other way too. This is just to secure your sticks – the fun part of decorating comes next.

3. You will need some patience for this part, as even for older children this is quite a challenging and time-consuming process, but it is also soothing and therapeutic. Using your first colour of wool, start working around your X by wrapping a loop around each stick, then turn, wrap a loop around the next stick, turn and repeat until you have built up that colour as much as you like and are ready for the next colour.

4. When you are ready to switch colours, cut the colour you are working on, leaving a dangling thread.

5. Take a new colour and knot together the two colours. Position the knot to be in the back of the god's eye and begin repeating the action of looping around each stick, turn, wrap a loop around the next stick, turn and repeat until you have either achieved the size god's eye you are happy with or are ready to switch colours again.

6. Once you're finished with your god's eye, wind your final loop around a stick, cut your wool and knot it around the stick. Add a second knot on the same stick just to be sure that your wool is secure and won't unravel.

7. Hang and display your god's eye with pride.

Fire lighting

Fire has been such a major part of life for millennia and it's so important that children learn to respect fire from an early age and that they are carefully taught how to properly start and manage them. It's imperative that any fire lighting is managed in a way that keeps children and adults safe and also protects the natural environment. Many public areas do not allow fires, so this is an activity that will work better in your garden. Even there, make sure the conditions are not hot and dry before lighting a fire as sparks can travel further than you would imagine. Protect your children and preserve the natural world.

Natural resources required:

- ♦ Four sticks to create a 1-metre boundary
- ♦ **Completely dry** kindling – small twigs and bark (silver birch is good, make sure any kindling sticks are completely dry – if you snap them, you should hear a clear snap)
- ♦ **Completely dry** medium sticks/chopped firewood to maintain a fire. Preferably seasoned or kiln dried.

Also required:

- ♦ Cotton wool ball or pads
- ♦ Flint and steel fire striker
- ♦ Bucket of water
- ♦ Fire safety glove

Optional resources:

- ♦ Metal bowl (if the ground isn't suitable for lighting a fire on)
- ♦ Marshmallows

1. Begin by creating a safety zone around your potential fire. Ensure the area you are planning to set your fire lighting activity in is free of any flammable materials. This includes any dried leaves, sticks, clothing, fabric. Your fire safety zone should be completely clear.

2. Once the area is completely cleared, ensure you have at least a ½-metre (20-in) square safety zone (if lighting a very small fire contained in a small bowl; increase to a

minimum of 1 metre/3 feet if a larger fire) around your fire. It must only ever be located within your safety zone and children must not enter the safety zone without an adult's permission and close supervision.

3. The second step of the necessary safety precautions is to fill a bucket with water. It's important to discuss with your child why you are doing this and why it's important to ensure you are safe working with fire.

4. The third step is a reminder of the safety rules for body positioning around a fire. Always take the safety position when kneeling near a fire, which is one knee up and one knee down. This keeps you more balanced and less likely to fall.

5. Before you build and attempt to light a fire, spend some time practising with a flint and steel to try and create a spark. Encourage your child to experiment with which hand feels more comfortable holding the flint and which the steel. To create a spark, keep the flint tilted forwards and then scrape hard and fast against the steel, always away from your body. This is far more challenging than it sounds, so encourage your child to persist and show perseverance as they work towards making a spark.

6. Once you have mastered the art of creating a spark using a fire striker, it's time to add some fuel to this to complete the fire triangle of IGNITION – OXYGEN –

FUEL. Cotton wool is a great material to use as tinder, the initial fuel to get a fire going. Take a cotton wool pad or ball and tease it out, fluffing out all of the fibres. The fibres are what will catch your spark and light, so you need as many of them sticking up as possible. Place it in the fire area.

7. Repeat the exercise of creating a spark with the flint and steel, this time angled towards your cotton wool; persevere until a spark lights it. Continue this exercise with more cotton wool, ensuring you continue at all times to follow all safety precautions.

8. Once you have mastered the art of lighting your cotton wool, it's time to build the next phase. Set up some cotton wool, as previously, but this time carefully and delicately add some peeled bark and kindling twigs. You want just enough to initially feed the fire, without too many twigs weighing down the cotton wool and not allowing any oxygen in. Place smaller, lighter pieces of bark on top and around your cotton wool, then stack any twigs in a pyramid shape around it. Less is more at this stage.

9. Using your cotton wool lighting skills, ignite the cotton wool again and this time watch it catch the bark or twigs alight. You may need to blow the fire gently to increase the initial flames. I recommend this job is initially carried out by an adult until you feel your child can do this safely.

10. When the fire has caught, using your fire glove feed the fire from the side, continuing to use small twigs and sticks until the fire is established, at which point you can add medium or larger sticks.

11. Once your fire is established and burning well, it's a good time to toast a marshmallow. Sliding a marshmallow onto the end of a thin stick, rotate it carefully in the flame, then when you pull it out of the flame, count to 10 before eating it to ensure you don't burn your mouth.

12. When your fire-lighting activity is over, regardless of whether the fire looks as though it has gone out, model good fire practice to your child by pouring over your bucket of water, slowly working from the outside to the centre of the fire to ensure it is completely extinguished.

Cooking on the fire

Once you have mastered the art of fire lighting, you can progress to cooking on the fire. There's something primordial about cooking on a fire, and it's something children enjoy as much as adults.

You can get as elaborate as you like cooking on the fire, but here are my children's favourite recipes.

DAMPER BREAD

There are so many recipes for this. We keep it simple and easy to prepare as I find you are far more forgiving of a food that you've cooked over the fire!

Ingredients:

- ♦ 1 tsp dried yeast
- ♦ 1 tbsp brown sugar
- ♦ 300 g (2.5 cups) flour
- ♦ 200 ml warm water
- ♦ 2 tbsp olive oil
- ♦ ½ tsp salt

1. In a large bowl add the dried yeast, brown sugar, flour, warm water, olive oil and salt.

2. The mix doesn't need kneading or any special treatment, just mix it all together using clean hands for a sensory experience or a wooden spoon. Leave the dough to rise while you build your fire.

3. Find some sticks to cook your damper bread on. If possible, peel your sticks a little and then hold them in the flame to sterilise a little and to pre-warm.

4. Taking a handful of dough from the mix, roll the dough in your hands into a sausage shape and then start winding it around a stick.

5. Once it is all safely attached, hold the stick in the fire and keep rotating the bread until it is uniformly coloured and sounds hollow when you tap it.

6. If you can manage to do this, slide out the stick to leave your damper bread hollow and fill with honey or jam.

BANANAS AND CHOCOLATE

Ingredients:
- Ripe bananas
- Chocolate callets

1. Take a ripe unpeeled banana and slice it open along one edge, just enough to push a handful of chocolate callets inside.

2. Once you have enough chocolate callets inside your banana, push the skin closed again and wrap tightly in foil.

3. Using some tongs, place the banana into the embers of your fire and turn once after five minutes.

4. Once it has been cooking for 10 minutes, pull your banana out of the fire using tongs and let it cool for a few minutes before opening the foil and enjoying.

Make a log or stone pet

This activity was created by my daughter when she was five years old and was still being played more than five years later! She used to name her 'pets' and they would travel everywhere with her for a while. She especially enjoyed putting homemade collars and leads made from twine on them, and taking them for walks.

Resources needed:
- Large log or stone
- Acrylic paint pens

Optional resource:
- Twine

Optional inspirational read:
- *Lesser Spotted Animals* by Martin Brown

1. Simply find an interesting-shaped large stone or log.

2. Using your acrylic pens, draw a face and animal features onto your new pet.

3. If you like, use twine to create a collar and lead and you can even take your pet for a walk.

Wormery

Worms are the most amazing creatures, and play such an important role in enriching soil and recycling nutrients. It's a great idea to make your kids aware of worms and to encourage them to inhabit your garden. Just be careful not to touch worms with your hands or you will hurt them. My children like to angle two small twigs next to each other and use these to carefully lift up the worms to relocate them.

Natural resources needed:

- Soil
- Sand
- Dead leaves
- Worm food – vegetable peelings, fresh leaves or grated carrot
- Earthworms

Also required:

- Large glass jar with air holes poked through the lid
- Black cardboard
- Water spray bottle

Optional inspirational reads:

- *Wiggling Worms at Work* by Wendy Pfeffer
- *Yucky Worms* by Vivian French

1. Fill your jar with alternating layers of soil, sand and dead leaves, dampening each layer using water from the spray bottle before you add the next.

2. Once you are nearly at the top, stop layering and add food for your worms to the top of your jar.

3. Put two to three earthworms into the jar and screw the lid on.

4. Earthworms prefer the dark, so wrap black cardboard around the jar and leave the worms in a warm place. Depending on the weather this could be outdoors or in colder weather you can bring them indoors. Don't place worms next to radiators or in an airing cupboard as you don't want to overheat them. Open the cardboard once a day to see if your worms have started burrowing around and mixing up the layers of your wormery.

5. After a week or so of observation, make sure to set your worms free again. Gently use a stick or tongs to remove them if they get stuck to the jar. The remaining mixture in your jar could by now be a fabulous compost to use for planting.

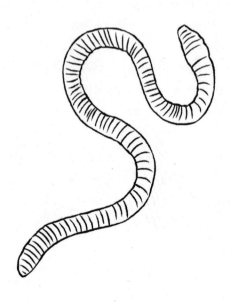

Build a den

Building dens and shelters is something that both adults and children really enjoy. It feels like using survival skills as well as role play and is a great problem-solving exercise where you need to collaborate and work as a team. There's something really rewarding about creating a shelter that you can then sit inside. It feels like a real achievement.

Natural resources needed:

- Long thick sticks
- Bendy branches
- Pine cones
- Bark
- Moss
- Grass
- Dried leaves

Optional resources:

- Tarpaulin (to make your den fully waterproof)

1. Look for a tree that you can use as a base for your den. You could seek out a tree with a thick trunk that'll be easy to lean sticks up against. Or a tree with a fork in the branches low enough to the ground that you can place sticks in it and have them reach the ground.

2. Gather up all of your large sticks and start to make a frame. I find myself often in these situations being a gatherer of sticks for my children as they manage the den construction.

3. Begin to make the frame of your shelter by leaning your sticks, pushing them securely into the ground and into the fork of the tree or against the tree to ensure you have a stable frame, built in the shape of a teepee. Don't forget to leave a space for an entrance.

4. Once you have a stable frame, you can start weaving
    bendy sticks horizontally if you want to add more
    substantial walls. My children love to make the walls
    more camouflaged by adding dried leaves, bark, moss
    and grass – pretty much anything they can find on the
    forest floor gets woven in and they often use mud for
    cement.

5. Finish off your den with a carpet of dry leaves inside and
    then crawl in to let the role play begin. Your children,
    as always, will have the best ideas for this. We've played
    castles and knights, tea parties, mummies and daddies,
    shops, cafes and even Warrior Cats. The list is endless.

Stick sculptures

I've spent hours in the forest with my children using sticks and the nature around them to create natural art. You can use sticks to make a life-size 2-D dinosaur, create a stick 'spider's web', form giant flowers out of sticks and leaves, and much more.

Natural resources needed:

- ◆   Selection of sticks
- ◆   Bark or leaves

Optional inspirational read:

- ◆   *Black Artists Shaping the World* by Sharna Jackson

1.   When walking around the forest, look for and collect some unusually shaped sticks, branches or twigs.

2.   Lay out the sticks and see what sort of creatures or creations spring to mind. Use the sticks to form the shape of these creatures on the ground.

3.   Use other natural materials to infill the creation – colourful leaves, stones, flowers and feathers all help to add depth and beauty to the artwork.

4. When children have finished making their animal shapes or other artistic creations, help them to find a name for their artwork.

5. If your children have made a few sculptures, you can even be invited by them to visit their art gallery and walk around their art installations, asking questions about what inspired them to create their beautiful creations.

Acorn fairy tea party

From a young age children love role playing tea parties with teddies, friends and fairies. This takes your tea party and turns it into a lovely outdoor activity, rich in imagination, fine motor skills and creativity.

Natural resources needed:

♦ Acorns
♦ Flowers
♦ Leaves
♦ Bark
♦ Tiny twigs
♦ Pebbles

Optional resource:

♦ Hot glue gun or craft glue

Optional inspirational read:

♦ *The Tea Party in the Woods* by Akiko Miyakoshi

1. Collect lots of natural resources and prepare to set up a delicious tea party. As always, children will have far better ideas than adults in this set-up.

2. In the past we've used pieces of bark to form a table, flat pebbles to be chairs around the table, set with tiny twig cutlery, acorn tea cups and leaf plates with petal cakes.

3. Experiment with setting up a tea party for fairies, for elves, teddy bears or for any creatures you can imagine may want to come along and join your tea party.

Create leaf art

Often the greatest beauty comes from the simplest of places. Take some time to notice and enjoy the changing seasons with your children.

Natural resources required:

♦ Beautiful autumn leaves

Optional inspirational read:

♦ *Leaf Man* by Lois Ehlert

1. Collect some autumn leaves. Throw them in the air and see how they land. Can you see any shapes in the leaves? Some leaves may look like beautiful animals, some may group together to form recognisable shapes.

2. If you want to extend this activity you can stick the leaves onto paper in their shapes, but often this is a fun game just for the physical, sensory fun of throwing leaves accompanied by the excitement and inspiration created by spotting shapes in the way they land.

Leaf mandala

A mandala is an abstract design usually circular in shape. Have you ever considered making a leaf mandala? It doesn't only need to contain leaves, so see what other gorgeous natural treasures you can find at a time of year when we are surrounded by beautiful colours. My children love making spiral shapes with their mandalas.

Natural resources required:

♦   Beautiful autumn leaves

1. Find a clear patch of grass or pavement on which to create your mandala art.

2. Choose a special leaf or another of your natural treasures to act as your focus and place it in the centre of the space.

3. Using your leaves or another natural treasure, start to make a spiral, moving ever further away from your central focus.

4. Step back to take a look at your mandala from a distance. You've created a beautiful piece of art that will undoubtedly brighten up someone's day when they walk by.

Conkers

Often an activity in itself is to collect conkers. My children love collecting ... pretty much anything. Our house is full of special stones, sticks, pine cones and conkers that they can personally identify from a couple of metres away. Indulge your inner collector and see how many conkers you can collect in a week.

Conkers are a fabulous addition to your household supplies as they can be used in a multitude of ways, from maths games to representing people/cars/animals in role play. You can even transform them by adding additional features through craft activities.

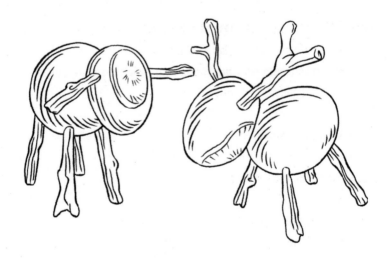

As these are such gems for the household, we often go over the top and collect far too many. If this is you too, there is an easy way to preserve them. Take the conkers that you aren't planning to use for crafts (remove the outer spiky shell if it has one), and pop them on a baking tray to bake for two–three hours at 140°C/275°F in the oven. This not only magically hardens them but stops them from going mouldy. We have some four-year-old baked conkers in our house, still going strong.

Optional inspirational reads:
- *October, October* by Katya Balen
- *Tree: Seasons Come, Seasons Go* by Patricia Hegarty and Britta Teckentrup

CONKER NECKLACES

Resources needed:
- Palm drill
- Conkers
- Twine

1. Using a palm drill, carefully drill a hole through each of your conkers.

2. Once you have enough conkers, thread them all onto a string and make a necklace. What a lovely gift!

CONKER ART

You may have seen this activity with marbles, which are also fun, but conkers are even better!

Resources needed:
- ◆ Old cardboard packaging box
- ◆ Paper
- ◆ Brightly coloured paints
- ◆ Conkers

1. Place a sheet of paper on the bottom of a cardboard box and then squeeze out 2–3 blobs of different colour paints.

2. Throw a handful of conkers into the box then tilt your box from side to side so that the conkers roll through the paint and create fabulous, Jackson Pollock-style art.

CONKER HEDGEHOGS AND OTHER CREATURES

Conkers are great for using to create little creatures!

Resources needed:

- ◆ Acrylic pens
- ◆ Dry leaves
- ◆ Twine
- ◆ Toothpicks
- ◆ Conkers!

1. Push toothpicks into the top of a conker to form the quills of your conker hedgehog and draw on a face.

2. Using toothpicks, dry leaves, twine and acrylic pens, challenge your child – what conker creatures can they design?

Pine cone animals

Another coveted collector's item in our home is pine cones.
My children love to collect all different sizes and shapes.
I have pockets, handbags and hats full of pine cones after
every walk through a pine forest. My youngest daughter can
spend hours delightfully and painstakingly picking off the sap,
whereas my other children are far happier using the cones in
craftmaking.

Again, we often go over the top and collect far too many.
If this is you too, there is an easy way to preserve them. Fill
a large bowl or a bucket with half hot water and half vinegar.
Soak the pine cones in the mixture for 45 minutes, stirring
every 10–15 minutes. Remove the pine cones and leave them
to air dry on a large towel for a couple of days. They will dry

quicker if they are near a radiator but don't place them on the radiator. Once they are dry, they will have opened up again and all of the sap will be gone.

Natural resources needed:

- Pine cones

Also required:

- Hot glue gun or craft glue
- Felt pieces
- Lollipop sticks
- Paint brush
- Acrylic paints
- Pipe cleaners
- Coloured wool
- Scrap cardboard

Optional inspirational reads:

- *The Last Tree* by Emily Haworth-Booth
- *The Giving Tree* by Shel Silverstein

1. Take a pine cone from your collection and step backwards. Turn it upside down, and then the right way round again. Does it remind you of anything? Does it look like an animal?

2. Decide what sort of creature you would like to turn your cone into. You can even make up a creature from your imagination if you would prefer.

3. Start to decorate the pine cone to create your creature.
    Use the glue to stick bits and pieces on to form arms and
    legs, noses, ears or anything you like!

4. Use paints, coloured wool and bits of paper to make fur
    or clothes or scales for your creature.

5. Why stop at one? You could make a whole family of pine
    cone friends to play with!

Animal face leaf masks

Autumnal colours are such a source of inspiration. We could play with the leaves for ever. This activity was inspired by some children in our nursery one day who were playing superheroes and were desperate for some masks. We used what we had and created such fabulous masks that the activity fast became a favourite.

Natural resources needed:
- Autumnal leaves

Also required:
- Cardboard
- Pen/pencil
- Scissors
- Stick or ribbon
- Glue stick/PVA glue
- Stick from the forest or a lollipop stick

Optional inspirational reads:
- *I Am The Seed That Grew The Tree* by Fiona Waters
- *Leaf* by Sandra Dieckmann

1. Draw out the outline shape of the mask that you want to use on cardboard, being as creative as you can, and cut it out. Measure up against your child to check where the eye holes should go and cut them out.

2. Go for a wander to see what leaves you can find for your mask. Aim for dry leaves as those with too much moisture won't stick to the mask.

3. Cover your cardboard mask in glue and start sticking the leaves on. Layering different coloured leaves on top of each other can look beautiful if you have the patience to wait for the first layer to dry.

4. Once you've completed your mask, decide how you want to use it. Would you like to hold it next to your face with a stick at the base or tie it on? If you want to tie it on, make two small holes at either side and attach two pieces of ribbon. These can then be tied around your child's head. If you'd prefer to use a stick, glue your stick to the back of the mask. To make it more secure, add a couple of pieces of ribbon to secure the stick to the mask.

5. Make sure you wait for the glue to dry before holding your mask next to your face for the transformation.

Leaf printing and painting

We love leaf printing. At my school we have some gorgeous pieces of art work displayed made by children through printing using natural materials. After practising a few times with leaf printing, when you get the hang of it, you could work on leaf-print artworks which make the perfect gift for a friend or family member. Leaf prints also make lovely cards, for Christmas, birthdays, or just to share that you are thinking of someone.

Natural resources needed:
- Autumnal leaves

Also required:
- Paper or cardboard
- Paintbrush
- Paint pallet/piece of cardboard
- Seasonal coloured paint – we like yellow and red

Optional inspirational reads:
- *Mix It Up!* by Hervé Tullet
- Woodland Trust *Leaf Swatch Book*

1. Take a walk and look for some leaves. You want flat leaves that haven't curled up yet as they will provide a clearer print. Ideally you are looking for fairly dry leaves for the best paint results.

2. Start by creating your colours: three to four colours are ideal. You have red and yellow as two primary colours, so you could try mixing up two different shades of orange to add some fun colour mixing to the activity. Experiment with the different shades you can make by slowly adding and mixing more red into your yellow. If you don't have a pallet, it's easy to mix small amounts of paint on a piece of cardboard.

3. Once you have your colours mixed and ready to use, choose your favourite leaves. Turn the leaf upside down and paint the bumpy side of the leaf, carefully covering all of the veins thoroughly in paint.

4. Press the painted leaf firmly down onto your paper or card, being careful not to move it once it's on the paper to make sure you get a clear print.

5. Once you have pressed the leaf onto the paper, gently peel the leaf away to reveal the print.

6. Repeat this process with different-sized leaves and different paint colours until your artwork is finished.

Mud faces on trees

This is a great activity that allows children to indulge in creativity and also be a bit spooky. It's a fun thing to do around Halloween and it's easy to encourage a little competition among siblings to create the scariest faces! It's equally lovely to just try and make beautiful woodland animals to decorate the forest.

Natural resources required:

♦   Mud
♦   Sticks
♦   Acorns, leaves, flowers, stones, feathers, etc.

1. Look for some nice damp mud for this activity and take a look around to see what trees you can turn into tree monsters or tree animals.

2. Scoop up a nice handful of mud and if it's dry enough, roll it into a semi-ball before pushing onto a tree. If it's too squelchy for that, slop the mud straight onto the tree in a circular shape. If the soil is too dry where you are, try pouring a little of your drinking water into a pile of mud to see if you can achieve the consistency you need.

3. Before your mud dries, start pushing some sticks, leaves, acorns, flowers or stones into your mud masks to form faces of mud monsters. If you want to challenge yourself further, make mud animals on the trees for each other and see if you can guess each other's animals.

6.

Activities for Winter

Natural winter tree decorations

I love that in the UK we are lucky enough to experience four distinct seasons. I love watching the seasons change and all that adapts in nature during each season. Winter is a magical time, but as the natural world beds down we can often lose colour in our world. My children and I love to use natural resources to make winter decorations to hang from our tree to brighten up our winter world.

Optional inspirational reads:

- *Eco Girl* by Ken Wilson-Max
- *The Winter Tree* by Stuart James
- *Tree: Seasons Come, Seasons Go* by Patricia Hegarty and Britta Teckentrup

PAINTED STAR DECORATION

This is a very simple activity that results in beautifully bright winter decorations. We love to make a few of these at a time.

Natural resources needed:

- Sticks

Also required:

+ Paintbrush
+ Paints
+ String or wool
+ Hot glue gun or craft glue

1. Select three fairly dry sticks of similar sizes for each star – we usually aim for approximately 8 cm (3 in) long sticks/twigs – and arrange them across each other to get an idea of star shapes you want to make. Separate into piles.

2. Once you have the piles of sticks ready, select your paint colours. How do you want your stars to look? Do you want different coloured sticks in one star or sticks all the same colour? Carefully paint your sticks in their groups of three in the colours you would like and let them dry.

3. When your sticks are dry to the touch, glue the sticks to each other in the star shape you practised earlier. Let your glue dry so the star is secure.

4. Using string or wool, tie a loop around the top of one of the star's sticks so you can hang it from your Christmas tree or chosen outdoor tree. Or indeed anywhere else that needs a boost of colour.

THREADED ORANGE SLICES AND CINNAMON

This is a great activity for practising fine motor skills and I love it as it makes the house smell delicious.

Natural resources needed:

- Oranges
- Cinnamon sticks

Also required:

- String
- Oven
- Tea towel/kitchen towel

Optional natural resources:

- If any of your previously collected conkers or pine cones are going spare, they will look great on these decorations

1. Firstly, slice the oranges into approximately 5 mm (¼ in) thick slices. Large oranges will be easier to work with, so find the biggest you can.

2. Preheat the oven to 100°C/212°F, first removing the oven racks.

3. Lay all the orange slices on a tea towel or some kitchen towel and pat gently with kitchen towel on top. You are aiming to remove as much moisture as you can, without damaging the flesh of the orange.

4. Place your orange slices directly onto the oven racks so the air can circulate freely around them. Place back in the warm oven and bake for around three hours. After the first hour check the orange slices as they sometimes fall off the rack and need to be popped back on.

5. After the first hour check every 30 minutes that they aren't burning, in which case turn the oven off.

6. Once three hours have passed, turn off the oven but leave the orange slices in there to continue to dry out for another hour. Make sure you remember to take them out before you turn on the oven to start cooking the next meal – I've accidentally burnt my oranges a few times through forgetting to remove them from the oven!

7. Once your orange slices are dry, push a hole through the flesh at the top of each slice to prepare for threading.

8. Cut a length of string to 20–30 cm (8–12 in), depending upon the size of decoration you are making. Tie a knot at one end of the string then thread a slice of orange and tie another knot to ensure the orange doesn't slip.

9. Leaving a space of approximately 2.5 cm (1 in), place a cinnamon stick on your string. Wrap the string securely around the stick, again knotting either end.

10. Repeat in whatever pattern you would like, interspersing your orange slices and cinnamon sticks with conkers and pine cones, if you like, until you have your final decoration ready to be hung.

STICKS IN THE SHAPE OF A TREE

I love the simplicity of this decoration. We make these small enough to hang on a tree, but have in the past made large-scale versions which we have hung as Christmas trees, both at school and at home.

Natural resources needed:

♦ Sticks

Also required:

♦ Hot glue gun

♦ String

Optional resources:

♦ Mini pompoms or other decorations like star stickers

♦ Paint and paintbrush

♦ Christmas baubles

♦ Pine cones

♦ Battery-operated fairy lights

SMALL HANGING DECORATION

1. To make a small, hanging tree decoration, go for a walk and bring back some thin sticks that you will be able to snap into pieces. You will need to end up with approximately eight to nine sticks.

2. Start with your first and largest stick (ideally approximately 10–13 cm/4–5 in long) and lay it flat on the table/floor in front of you. Then snap a second stick a couple of centimetres or so shorter and place it on the table above and touching your first stick.

3. Repeat this with your remaining sticks, working your way up to smaller and smaller sticks, until your snapped sticks form a triangle shape.

4. Using either a lollipop stick or a long, flat stick from the forest as a spine for your tree, hot glue this spine stick to your triangle of sticks in order of largest to smallest.

5. Tie your string into a loop from which you can hang your decoration and then hot glue your string to the spine stick.

6. Let the hot glue dry until the sticks are secure, then either hang the tree as it is or decorate it. My children love to decorate with mini pompoms to represent baubles and place a star sticker at the top. Let your imagination run wild – you could even paint on decorations.

7. Once fully dry, hang it up on your tree.

LARGE WALL DECORATION

If you're opting to make this homemade version of the expensive stick Christmas trees you may have seen in boutique shops, it's a similar process to making the small hanging decoration and you need the same resources.

1. Go for a walk and bring back some sticks and twigs of varying sizes. If they are wet, leave them somewhere to dry for a couple of days before making your Christmas tree.

2. When your sticks are dry, arrange them on the floor in order of size, with the longest closest to you (on the bottom) up to the smallest furthest from you (the top), to form a triangular shape (it should look like a Christmas tree!). Each stick should be approximately 20 cm (8 in) apart.

3. Take three long pieces of string. Working from the top down, tie one piece of string to one end of the shortest stick, and another on the other end. Then tie a third piece of string in the middle of the shortest stick.

4. Take each piece of string straight down to the next biggest stick and wrap each of them (keeping them as separate lines of string) around the centre and outside edges of the stick and tie another knot to secure. Once your string is secure, take each piece of string down to the next largest stick, wrap them around and tie a knot to secure the stick.

5. Repeat this process working down from smallest to largest, ensuring you leave an even gap (approximately 20 cm/8 in) between each stick, until you reach the bottom and all of your sticks are now attached to your three lines of string.

6. Cut a new piece of string, double it over for additional strength and make a double-thickness loop around your top stick to allow you to hang the Christmas tree.

7. Once your Christmas tree is ready and hung, you can hot glue some pine cones, Christmas baubles or even your own homemade decorations to the tree and maybe decorate the finished product with battery-operated fairy lights.

Acorn jewellery for winter gifts

These make lovely gifts for friends and family. It's a bit of a fiddly craft that needs adult support but is also really rewarding for the beautiful result. I've been the lucky recipient of a few acorn necklaces in my time.

Natural resources needed:

♦   Acorn caps

Also required:

♦   Drill
♦   Jewellery cord/string/ribbon
♦   Hot glue gun or craft glue
♦   Salt dough (1 cup of plain flour, ½ cup of salt, ½ cup of water) to make 'jewels'
♦   Paintbrush
♦   Paint

Optional resources:

♦   Glass marbles
♦   Superglue

1.   Your first task is to head out on a nature hunt to gather together as many acorn caps as you can find. Sometimes drilling into acorn caps can break them, so picking up some spare can be helpful. Larger acorn caps will allow you to make larger pendants.

2.   Set out your acorn caps in order of size. An adult will need to use the finest drill bit possible and drill a hole sideways through the acorn cap.

3.   Thread your jewellery cord, string or ribbon through the drilled holes from one side to the other to create a pendant.

4. To make sure that my matching caps and 'jewels' (once made!) stay together, I usually lay out my acorn caps on a sheet of paper inside circles, labelled by number.

5. Preheat the oven to 60–80°C (140–176°F) and line a baking tray with baking paper. Draw corresponding circles to your caps on the baking paper, labelled by number.

6. Make a salt dough by stirring together the flour, salt and water until it comes together in a ball. With floured hands roll out small balls to form the jewels in your pendants, testing them against your chosen acorn caps to ensure they will fit snugly inside.

7. When you have finished making them, place each jewel into the corresponding circle on your baking paper and pop the tray into the oven for approximately three hours.

8. Depending on how many pendants you have made, you will have some salt dough left over so on a floured surface you could make some dough jewellery holders or just shapes – my children love rolling out largeish flat circles, pinching up the sides to form a lip and then making hand prints in which to hold treasures. Once completed, these will need to join your jewels in the oven.

9. Once your jewels have baked and cooled, it's time to paint them. We find painting with lots of different colours works best. Or to achieve a marbled effect my daughter likes to fill an egg cup with different coloured paints in layers. Then she dips her salt dough in and pulls it out gently.

10. Let your jewels dry, then attach to the acorn caps using hot or craft glue. If you would like to secure these even more you can use superglue but this must be carried out by an adult.

11. As an alternative, we have seen friends glue glass marbles into acorn caps to make their pendants. This achieves an equally beautiful result if you don't want to play with and bake salt dough. Gift these to lucky recipients.

Frozen suncatchers to hang in trees

Sometimes on really cold days you need to wrap up warm and find the inspiration to head outdoors to play. This is such a lovely thing to create – and it embraces the cold! It also offers great follow-up activities as you observe the transformation from icy suncatcher back to natural treasures.

Natural resources needed:

- Sticks, pine cones, leaves, petals, berries, grasses

Also required:

- Water
- Container to freeze water in (cleaned yogurt pot/ silicone cake mould/plastic bowl – whatever you have available)
- String or ribbon
- Drill

Optional resources:

- Food colouring

Optional inspirational read:

- *A Dot in the Snow* by Corrinne Averiss

1. Firstly, gather up some interesting looking items. If you can find anything colourful, it will help to make your suncatcher even more interesting.

2. Pour some water into your container, then arrange your treasures decoratively in the water. Leave a clear space to drill a hole through later, or if you don't want to drill through ice, pop in something heavy like a stone that the water can freeze around leaving a hole for your string or ribbon.

3. Optional here, depending on whether the natural treasures you have found are colourful enough for you, is to add some spots of food colouring to the water.

4. Depending on how cold it is outside, you can either pop this in the freezer to freeze or, as we prefer to do, leave the container outside as there's something more magical about it turning into an icy suncatcher from being left on a windowsill outside overnight.

5. When the water has frozen, pop your icy suncatcher out of its container, drill a hole through the suncatcher if you need to, then thread through it with string or ribbon. Hang it up in the sunshine to see it swing and the sun shine through your beautiful decoration.

6. This is a great opportunity for hypothesising and experimenting with your suncatcher. It looks amazing hanging in the sun, but does it melt more slowly if you hang it in the shade? Does it melt faster if you are touching it with your warm hands? Do dark leaves melt at the same rate as lighter coloured leaves? Enjoy your scientific experiments!

Colourful snow art

If you are lucky enough to experience snow during winter, then this is a fabulous opportunity for so much play.

Natural resources needed:
- Snow

Also required:
- Food colouring (gel style food colourings are less fun to work with but have a richer colour)
- Spray bottles (we use old cleaning bottles for this, with all cleaning labels pulled off and clearly relabelled as play bottles to avoid confusion)

Optional resources:
- Pipettes
- Tray

Optional inspirational read:
- *Wolf in the Snow* by Matthew Cordell

1. Fill some spray bottles with water and add a few drops of food colouring at a time until you achieve the depth of colour you would like. This is an interesting experiment

in dilution, while using pipettes is great for fine motor skills.

2. Once you've achieved the colour of water you hoped for, head outside with your spray bottles, find a pile of snow or create a big ball of it and start squirting. Create a masterpiece!

Icy discoveries

My children, being children, love activities where toys are revealed. Often in toys you purchase this means eggs covered in excessive plastic, which is just so bad for the environment and so wasteful. What I've described here is such a fun way to reveal toys, doesn't require buying mounds of plastic, and is an activity which enthrals children for such a long time.

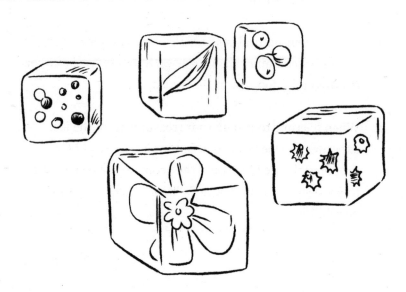

Natural resources needed:

♦ Flowers, leaves, conkers

Other resources needed:

♦ Water, containers

Optional resources:

♦ Lego men or toy dinosaurs

Optional inspirational read:

♦ *Ice is Nice! All about the North and South Poles* by Bonnie Worth

1. Choose your natural or other resources and pop each one into a container then cover with water. Freeze either overnight outdoors or in the freezer.

2. When it's time to rescue your treasures from the ice, experiment. Does leaving it out in the sun work? Or dropping the ice block onto the ground? Maybe you want to use a stone to chisel away? There are so many fun possibilities!

Make your own broomstick

The forest can look bare in the depths of winter, when most flowers and other colour has faded away for the winter.
Use the natural resources still available by selecting lots of dry, bare sticks and twigs to make your very own witch's or wizard's broomstick.

Natural resources needed:
♦   One large stick, lots of smaller twigs and sticks

Also required:
♦   String

Optional resources:
♦   Paintbrush
♦   Paint

Optional inspirational reads:
♦   *Meg and Mog* by Helen Nicoll
♦   *Room on the Broom* by Julia Donaldson

1.   Lay out your large stick and gather your smaller twigs and sticks around one end to form a natural broomstick.

2. Wrap your string around the twigs to create at least an 8-cm (3-in) section of string securing the sticks to the broomstick handle.

3. As an optional activity you can paint your broomstick handle or sticks for decoration.

4. Hop onto your broomstick and fly away to create some magic!

Homemade bird feeders

We love to support the wildlife in our garden and offer our
birds an easy way to get the food they need to keep warm
through the colder days.

Natural resources needed:

- Pine cones

Also required:

- 200–250g (7–9 oz) bird seed mix
- 2–4 tablespoons raisins, pre-soaked in water
- 50g (2 oz) lard
- 50g (2 oz) natural peanut butter with no salt added
  (if you have an allergy, substitute this with more
  lard)

◆ Cookie cutters
◆ Pencils
◆ Ribbon

Optional inspirational reads:
◆ *Snow Birds* by Kirsten Hall
◆ *Twitch* by M. G. Leonard

1. This is a really lovely sensory activity which is best mashed together with little hands, so wash hands and get messy. Melt the lard and peanut butter together until they are liquid, then stir in your bird seed until all of the seeds are coated in liquid. Stir in the raisins. Set aside to cool.

2. Prepare a baking tray with baking paper and get your cookie cutters ready. I like to rub some lard around the inside of them to make the feeders easier to remove.

3. Once your mixture is ready, press it into your cookie cutters until it is packed tightly. Using a pencil, push a hole through the top of your bird feeder decoration ready to thread your string or ribbon through.

4. Once you have used all of the mix, place the baking tray in the fridge and leave to set for at least three hours. If you have time, leave the feeders in there overnight to really dry out.

5. Remove the feeders from the fridge and gently remove
    them from the cookie cutters before threading with
    ribbon and hanging them up in a tree. We try to hang
    ours near a window so we can look out and see the birds
    feasting on our treats.

Edible winter tree decorations for wildlife

A few years ago we read the beautiful *Night Tree* book by Eve Bunting and thought it was such a lovely idea to decorate a tree to provide some winter treats for our local wildlife. We began making edible decorations and it has now become an annual tradition.

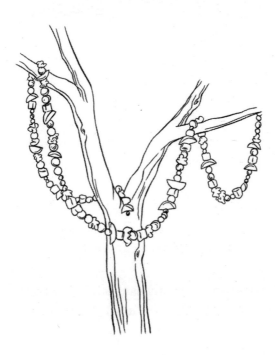

Resources needed:
- String or craft wire
- Apples and cheese, chopped into cubes
- Cranberries, cheerios, plain popcorn (not salt or sweet)

Optional inspirational read:
- *Night Tree* by Eve Bunting

1. Lay out all of the ingredients.

2. Decide upon how long each garland or hanging-loop edible decoration is going to be. We tend to aim for a short garland and small loops to give us the best chance of the decoration staying intact until it's used to decorate a tree.

3. Thread your chopped apple and cheese, cranberries, Cheerios and popcorn onto string in any combination that looks good to you.

4. Once all of your decorations are finished, head out into your garden or a local park and find a tree with low-hanging branches that you can reach.

5. Take some time to gently hang all of your edible decorations as a gift to the wildlife. We love to keep an eye on our tree and observe which birds and animals scamper along to enjoy our feast.

Bark rubbing

The next time you go out for an adventure walk, take some paper and crayons. Although this is a tactile activity, it's also easy to enjoy with gloves on – crucial for an activity on a cold winter's day!

Natural resources needed:

♦ Trees with interesting bark – bumpy and raised textures are best

Also required:

♦ Paper
♦ Crayons

Optional inspirational read:

♦ *The Little Book of Trees* by Caz Buckingham and Andrea Pinnington

1. As you walk, look at the trees you pass. Can you see any trees with interesting-looking bark?

2. When you find a tree you would like to sample, place your paper against the tree and then rub your crayon over the paper to capture the pattern of the bark.

3. It's fascinating to experiment with different colours for each type of tree and then to really look at the different bark patterns you've captured in just the small area of the outdoors you are exploring. We like to see if we can guess from the bark patterns on paper which tree we are working with and read more about the wonderful creatures that live on each tree.

4. Your bark rubbings can then be taken home and embellished with features that turn them into bark pattern characters.

Make a snow slide

We don't often get snow in London, but when we do, all else is abandoned to go and enjoy the fun. Nothing is more fun than sliding down snowy banks. If you don't have a suitably steep slope then you can pile up your snow to make yourself a slide.

Natural resources needed:
♦   Snow!

Also required:
♦   Cardboard or old packaging box
♦   Spray bottle of water

1. Pile layers of snow on top of one another. Stamp down hard between each layer to create a solid base for your slide.

2. Spray a little water on the slide if you'd like some added speed.

3. Find a piece of old cardboard or an old packaging box you can get inside and whizz down your slide!

Balancing on fallen trees

Balancing on fallen trees is such an open-ended activity that thrills children of all ages. On a walk, look out for fallen trees which offer opportunities for climbing, role play, scrambling, balancing ... the list is endless.

This is an excellent gross motor activity that develops a resilience, can-do attitude and teaches children to persevere and to take (safe) risks. It also develops proprioception, balance and coordination, all of which are essential for good physical development.

Natural resources needed:

♦ Fallen trees

1. Find your ideal fallen tree. Do check it for safety before allowing children to scramble over it. You want it to feel secure and not to roll when children climb it. (Never allow children to climb on log piles that have been created by storing large fallen logs and tree trunks together as they have the potential to roll and injure a child.)

2. If you have a tree that has fallen with a nice sturdy base, find yourself a nice place to sit as your child enjoys hours of fun.

Learn how to compost

It's so important to discuss with children how waste is managed where you live. We recycle all we can, but what happens to the landfill? It's important to minimise the waste you send to landfill as much as possible. At-home composting is a great way to reduce your waste while also creating conditions for growing your own fruit and vegetables.

A good way to start composting is to provide your child with their own compost system. This is a way to enable them to feel real ownership of their compost and to have a vested interest in observing the composting process.

Natural resources needed:
- Dead leaves, twigs and sticks
- Soil

Also required:
- Vegetable peelings
- Shredded newspaper
- Plastic 2-litre bottle

Optional inspirational reads:
- *The Kew Gardens Children's Cookbook* by Joe Archer and Caroline Craig
- *Compost Stew: An A-Z Recipe for the Earth* by Mary McKenna Siddals and Ashley Wolff
- *Climate Action* by Georgina Stevens

1. Take your 2-litre drink bottle, fix the lid tightly, remove any labels and clean the bottle so you are able to see inside it as the composting process works its magic.

2. Just below the neck of the bottle, cut approximately two-thirds of the way around the bottle to pull back and create a large opening, which you can then close.

3. You are going to layer your four layers of ingredients like a lasagne – soil; dead leaves; vegetable peelings and shredded newspaper. Try experimenting with different bottles to see which order works best. Does it make a difference which material you start with?

4. Once your bottle is full, tape up the large opening
    below the neck and place the compost bottle on a sunny
    windowsill. Keep an eye on the moisture level as you
    may need to spray a little water if the mixture gets
    too dry, or undo the lid to release some moisture if
    condensation forms on the inside of the bottle.

5. The composting process will take a few weeks. You can
    examine the bottle every few days to see if you can
    observe any changes, rolling the bottle around to mix
    the layers together.

6. Once the mixture looks brown, dry and crumbly, that's
    when your compost is ready. You can now marvel at the
    fact that you have processed your waste and turned it
    into something you can add to your garden to improve
    the quality of your soil, or save to use for planting your
    own seeds and growing your own vegetables.

Epilogue

The wild world is becoming so remote to children that they miss out – and an interest in the natural world doesn't grow as it should. Nobody is going to protect the natural world unless they understand it.

SIR DAVID ATTENBOROUGH

I hope this book has provided families with some inspiration to delve into engaging more as a family with the great outdoors. My dream with the creation of Little Forest Folk nurseries was always to support as many children to spend their childhood outdoors as possible.

By providing this generation with a deep love of and regular connection to nature, we are not only providing the foundation for a happy and healthy life for our young people, but are developing the future custodians of the planet.

The world we are living in is fast-paced, dynamic, exciting and challenging. Our young people need different skills to thrive than previous generations. By providing our young people with the opportunities that nature play affords, we develop the independent, self-confident, empathetic, resilient problem-solvers and critical thinkers of the future with a strong sense of social responsibility.

The future needs these skills. Not only for our children's path through school and careers, but for the benefit of society as a whole.

Appendix

RECOMMENDED CLOTHING BRANDS

Being warm and dry is the key to success for an outdoor adventure. It's worth spending money on as high-quality gear as possible. Facebook Marketplace or eBay are great places to find a bargain, as well as scouring charity shops if your network of friends and family providing hand-me-downs aren't as outdoorsy as you! With high-quality clothing and footwear you don't necessarily need to buy new as this is gear that will last.

Footwear

Vivo Barefoot: Lumi X for winter, Fulham boot for spring/autumn and Primus Sport or Ultra Bloom for summer. These are expensive but are so good, not just for foot health but the company has great environmental credentials too. This footwear lasts and has been handed down from child to child in my family. I love their ReVivo service where you can get footwear repaired, sell it on or return it so shoes and boots don't end up in landfill.

Thermals

Uniqlo

Marks & Spencer

Jumpers/fleece

Uniqlo

Frugi

Patagonia – I live in hope that their Worn Wear
programme will one day be extended to the UK. Until that
time, I try to buy second-hand as Patagonia clothing is very
good quality and will last. You don't need to buy this new.

Trespass

Jack Wolfskin

Polarn O. Pyret

Waterproofs

Didriksons

Hats and gloves

Jack Wolfskin

Babipur has a great selection

Polarn O. Pyret

RECOMMENDED SNACK AND FOOD EQUIPMENT

Yumbox – stainless steel

Ocean bottle

One green bottle

Thermos flask

Acknowledgements

I would like to thank all the wonderful people who have worked with me over the years at Little Forest Folk. You amaze me on a daily basis and have inspired so much of the nature play I enjoy with my children. The activities I recommend are only a handful of the joyful learning experiences I've witnessed you create in the forest. You are magical and committed professionals who work so hard to provide a childhood immersed in nature to the lucky Little Forest Folk children. Special thanks go to Lisa who was and remains a constant support in making the Little Forest Folk and now Liberty Woodland School magic happen.

My fantastic Liberty Woodland School teachers are the most skilled, hard-working, creative, kind and passionate educators I have ever met. They are utterly dedicated to providing children with an exemplary education which develops them into those young people most likely to succeed and thrive in school, careers and life. They also inspire and motivate me, our children and our entire school community to work hard for a better world for all. I count myself very lucky to work with you and am so grateful my children are being educated by you.

I'd also like to thank all of the educators around the world taking children regularly out into nature, come rain or shine. It's hard work, but so rewarding. The difference you make to children's lives by choosing this vocation is so appreciated.

Finally, my friends and family. It's been an outrageous journey over the past eight years to get us to where we are. The support of our family and friends has been invaluable. We couldn't have managed without you. Thanks to my mother especially, who brought me up to believe I can do anything.

My husband James joined me on this exciting and daunting journey, giving up his career temporarily to do so. It's been the hardest and best thing we've done together. Thank you for supporting me and helping to make this all possible, without losing sight of our family being the most important thing in the world.

To Ella, Jack and Indie. My inspiration, my life and my happy place. You are the reason Little Forest Folk and Liberty Woodland School exist. Thank you for teaching me what life is all about.

About the Author

Leanna entered the world of education after having her own children and wishing for a better learning environment for them. She founded Little Forest Folk from a dream to provide her children with the childhood they deserved. Her initial dream of one full-time forest nursery for her own children to attend was soon expanded through demand into an organisation of seven full-time nurseries, which have received numerous accolades, won many prizes and have been presented with an award from the Queen for innovation. Upon Leanna's children getting older, she began to pursue her dream of the creation of a primary school, then secondary school, that was an extension of the Little Forest Folk ethos. Liberty Woodland School is an academically rigorous school for the future, where 90 per cent of learning happens in nature. The focus is on allowing children to remain the individual wonders that they are as they progress through their school years, towards becoming those children most likely to succeed in today's world.

This is Leanna's first book.

For further information:
www.littleforestfolk.com
www.libertywoodlandschool.com

Notes

Notes

Notes